# FAITH, WORD AND CULTURE

*To Frank and Barbara Cain,*
*dedicated friends of the Pontifical Irish College*

Edited by Liam Bergin

# Faith, Word and Culture

the columba press

First published in 2004 by
the columba press
55A Spruce Avenue, Stillorgan Industrial Park,
Blackrock, Co Dublin


Cover by Bill Bolger
Origination by The Columba Press
Printed in Ireland by Betaprint, Dublin

ISBN 1 85607 445 5

# Table of Contents

# Introduction

The Second Vatican Council had a particular impact on the Irish College in Rome. The college was home to the Irish bishops and to the other *periti* that came from Ireland for the council. A photograph hangs in the college library of some sixty Irish-born bishops who were present for the last session of the council. From Ossory to Owerri, from Tuam to Tanga they converged on the city and on the college. Those who were students in the college during that period recall stories of the coming and goings, of the debates and controversies that spilled beyond Saint Peter's basilica, and of the sense of being present in Rome as an epoch-making event in the history of the church was underway.

In *Novo Millenio Ineunte*, in what is perhaps the most personal of his apostolic letters, Pope John Paul II encourages the church to face the third millennium 'in the light of the council'.

> With the passing of the years, the council documents have lost nothing of their value or brilliance. They need to be read correctly, to be widely known and taken to heart as important and normative texts of the magisterium, within the church's tradition. Now that the Jubilee has ended, I feel more than ever in duty bound to point to the council as the great grace bestowed on the church in the twentieth century: there we find a sure compass by which to take our bearings in the century now beginning.[1]

The fortieth anniversary of the opening of the Second Vatican Council, then, is not a matter of nostalgia or memory. Rather, it provides an opportunity to reassess the reception given to the council and to ensure that the direction that the church of the third millennium is taking is guided by that 'sure compass'.

Three of the papers in this book, together with their responses, were delivered at a conference on Vatican II held at the

---

1. *Novo Millenio Ineunte*, 57

Pontifical Irish College in May 2003. The conference, entitled
'Faith, Word and Culture', was one of a series of events held
during that year to celebrate the 75th anniversary of the building
of the present college. Since its foundations in 1628, the Irish
College has moved five times. The conference was made possible by the generous contribution of the Friends of the Pontifical
Irish College. A word of thanks is extended to all who supported
that event, particularly to Archbishop Michael Fitzgerald, the
President of the Pontifical Council for Inter Religious Dialogue,
Bishop John Fleming of Killala and Professor Ronan Drury, editor of *The Furrow*, who chaired the different lectures. These texts
are published not just to commemorate the opening of the
Second Vatican Council but to remind a new generation of
students of the enduring value of the 'normative texts' of the
council for the church of today.

*Liam Bergin*
*Rector*

# CHAPTER ONE

# Vatican II and the Status of Other Religions as Salvific Structures

## Gavin D'Costa

It is a great privilege and pleasure to be here to celebrate both the anniversaries of the Irish College and the documents of Vatican II. When I was here last in 1998, with my wife and two children as the Visiting McCarthy Professor at the Pontifical Gregorian University, we were enveloped in charming Irish hospitality that made our stay deeply memorable. The children practised repeated baptisms in the swimming pool. My very special thanks to the rector Mgr Bergin, who was then vice-rector, for the present invitation.

The question of the status of other religions has been around since the inception of Christianity, and what is so remarkable about Vatican II is that it is the first full ecumenical council to address this question in a rich, complex and most positive fashion. It opened the doors for the church to pursue a positive relation with other religions, as well as facilitating a great deal of theological discussion on a number of fronts. It has raised important trinitarian, ecclesiological and missiological issues, many of which have been so brilliantly addressed by theologians working in Rome, and at Fr Dan Madigan SJ's own Pontifical Gregorian University. One particular question that has been discussed with great passion is the question of the salvific status of other religions. I want to look at Vatican II and some post-Conciliar discussion to reflect further on this single issue.

*The Declaration on the Relationship of the Church to Non-Christian Religions (Nostra Aetate-NA)*, promulgated on October 28 in 1965, marked a decisive step in Roman Catholic theology of religions. In 1962 Pope John XXIII had personally requested Cardinal Bea to oversee the drafting of a statement on the Jews. This was to be have been chapter 4 of the schema of the *Decree on Ecumenism (Unitatis Redintegratio)*, but eventually mutated into a separate declaration on the world religions, not just Judaism. In the process the Secretariat for Non-Christian Religions was created in 1964 under Cardinal Marella. The Secretariat is now called the Pontifical Council for Interreligious Dialogue, and it is a great honour that the Prefect for the PCID, Archbishop Michael Fitzgerald, is here with us today. His special link with the Irish College, at least linguistically, is his shared name with the Jesuit Rector of the College from 1746-1750, Michael Fitzgerald! To return to our story, the resulting document on *Nostra Aetate* was both a miraculous triumph as well as a painful failure.

The triumph was at least twofold. First, as Cardinal Bea noted in introducing the final document, it was the first time that the church has made an official pronouncement regarding the non-Christian religions. The tone was entirely positive and the concern was to focus on what was held *in common* so as to build together from shared strengths. This was a gigantic step for the Roman Catholic Church. This is not the place to trace the earlier history on the question of other religions except to say that the traditional teaching *extra ecclesiam nulla salus* (no salvation outside the church) was never formulated or applied to non-Christian religions in the technical sense in which they are understood in the 1965 document, *Nostra Aetate*.[1] Thus was Leonard Feeney SJ ironically excommunicated in 1949 for refusing to retract his literal application of the *extra ecclesiam nulla salus* to those from other religions (and Protestants). He was pronounced *extra ecclesiam* for applying the *extra ecclesiam nulla salus* teaching to non-Catholics! Second, the Jewish question had allowed the African and Asian bishops to express concern about the invisibility of religions that partly formed their own cultures: Islam, African religions, Hinduism, and Buddhism. Many of the bishops in Arab and Muslim countries also feared Muslim reaction to a document exclusively on the Jews, in the light of the Middle East crisis. In consequence, the document addressed itself to the much wider question of relations with religions. However, the tragic counterpoint to this is the way in which the

1. See my '*Extra ecclesiam nulla salus* revisited', in ed. Ian Hamnett, *Religious Pluralism and Unbelief: Studies Critical and Comparative*, Routledge, London, 1990, 130-47, and Francis A. Sullivan, *Salvation Outside the Church?*, Geoffrey Chapman, London, 1992

original schema on the Jewish people was revised, finally failing to acknowledge Christian culpability in the long history of anti-Jewishness and the church's need for repentance and forgiveness. This step would eventually come under the present pontificate. Rabbi David Polish said of the document at the time that it was 'a unilateral pronouncement by one party which presumes to redress on its own terms a wrong which it does not admit.'[2]

In what follows I want to pursue a single question and one of the most important questions raised in the light of *Nostra Aetate*: are non-Christian religions, *per se*, vehicles of salvation? Can it be said that according to Vatican II non-Christian religions are mediators of supernatural revelation to their followers? This question absolutely takes for granted, following both pre-Conciliar and post-Conciliar teachings, that there is no doubt that the non-Christian may be saved. To answer my question, are non-Christian religions, *per se*, ever viewed as vehicles of salvation, I shall briefly inspect the Conciliar documents to see what kind of answer they give. I shall be arguing that they are silent, and this silence has in fact been read in two quite differing ways by post-Conciliar theologians. The types of readings, furthermore, are deeply affected by the presuppositions held by these theologians concerning nature and grace. Hence, there are theologians who argue that the documents affirm the possibility that non-Christian religions are means of supernatural revelation. These theologians tend to envisage a very close relationship between nature and grace. On the other hand, there are those who disagree and tend to envisage a sharper distinction between nature and grace. I will briefly try to show that the present Pope, John Paul II, is in the latter group of readers. He does not understand the documents to teach that non-Christian religions, *per se*, can be viewed as supernatural means to salvation or, as 'paths' to salvation. It is important to note that this finding is not a negative judgement upon non-Christian religions, but a theological affirmation of Christ's indissoluble relation to the church.

What does *Nostra Aetate* teach about other religions in terms of their being possible mediators of supernatural revelation and

2. Cited by Claud Nelson, 'A Response to *Nostra Aetate*', in Walter M. Abbot, *The Documents of Vatican II*, Guild Press, New York, 1966, 669-70

therefore salvation to their adherents? At least three things must be said in contextualising the silence that is found on this explicit question. First, the religions are seen to be differently related to the church in theological and historical terms: Judaism first, then Islam, and finally Hinduism, Buddhism, and 'other religions to be found everywhere' (*NA* 2). This latter phrase is taken to refer to 'primal' religions in Africa, although some argue that it should be extended to Shinto, Confucianism, and other Asian religions. In the official commentary, it is clear that these traditions cannot be regarded as monolithic entities, but such a brief pastoral document cannot enter into detailed historical descriptions. Judaism is seen as the root from which the church springs, out of 'Abraham's stock'. In this section we find the single exclusive use of the term *revelationem* (revelation) in regard to other religions, although the sentence in which the term is used refers to the 'Old Testament' so that it is difficult to speak of another religion bearing revelation *per se*. Rather it denotes what Christians view as revealed and sacred scripture – the Old Testament – as do Jews. The sentence reads: 'The church, therefore, cannot forget that she received the *revelation* of the Old Testament through the people with whom God in his inexpressible mercy deigned to establish the Ancient Covenant' (*NA* 4, my emphasis). It is worth noting that the term 'revelation' was not part of the original text, but was introduced in the second drafting, in September 1964 when the document was widened to refer to non-Christians. This is highly significant, for the term 'revelation' is not used in any of the sections dealing with other religions. This also highlights the *sui generis* relationship with Judaism, and implies that the non-use of the term 'revelation' regarding other religions can be seen as significant. Supernatural revelation is clearly related to Christ and Christian scripture, part of which is shared by the Jewish people. This is confirmed in *The Dogmatic Constitution on Divine Revelation* 14-16 *(Dei Verbum)*.

Second, *Nostra Aetate* is silent on the question of the salvation of the non-Christian. But this is not a silence, because it was not the remit of that document to address this specific question. For this question we must turn to *The Dogmatic Constitution on the Church*, 16 *(Lumen Gentium)*, and again we find a silence on the matter of the non-Christian religions *per se*, but not about the non-Christian's possible salvation. *Lumen Gentium* is unequivocal about the latter. The unique place of the Jews is acknowledged: 'the people to whom the covenants and promises were given.' Note that the document stops short of affirming the validity of Judaism *per se*. Islam, as in *Nostra Aetate*, is commended for its theism and belief in a creator God. However, it should be recalled that Vatican I already held that it was possible for women and men to come to knowledge of a creator God through the use of reason and in this respect, one does not have to impute supernatural salvific status to Islam as a religion, *per se*, by virtue of the fact that it is theistic.[3] This interpretation is supported by the fact that in the same section of *Lumen Gentium* the council fathers indicate that non-religious theists may 'sincerely seek God, and moved by his grace, strive by their deeds to do his will as it is known to them' (*LG* 16). Logically, this places non-religious theists in a similar category to Muslims regarding their theism, and this theism thereby logically requires no religious structure to mediate such belief.

Then, and this is most important, the council fathers make it clear that salvation can be attained by anyone, be they religious or not, whether they have explicit belief in God or not, under three conditions. First, that they 'through no fault of their own do not know the gospel of Christ or his church'. Second, that the non-culpable 'who have not yet arrived at an explicit knowledge of God, but who strive to live a good life, thanks to his grace' are not lost. When we ask how a person lives the good life, various conciliar documents give a uniform answer: through following one's conscience and the natural law that is written within the hearts of all and is part of the created order (see *Pastoral Constitution on the Church in the Modem World* 16, 29, [*Gaudium et Spes*]; *Declaration on Religious Freedom* 2, 3, [*Dignitatis Humanae*]; *Decree on the Church's Missionary Activity* 9, [*Ad Gentes*]). This is not supernatural revelation in the technical sense, although it is assisted by grace and leads to salvation. Third, these positive realities are but a preparation (*preparatio evangelica*) for the full

3. See *Dei Filius* (1870), esp. ch. 2; and the anathema in Denzinger 3026. Natural knowledge of God is also affirmed in *Dei Verbum*, 3, but carefully related in its function as a *preparatio evangelica*.

and undiminished truth of the gospel. This is explicitly stated in *Lumen Gentium* 16, with a note referring to Eusebius of Caesarae's *preparatio evangelica*. This is a restatement of the Thomistic principle: *gratia non tollit naturam, sed perficit* (grace does not destroy nature but perfects it).

All this indicates precisely what is said in *Nostra Aetate* regarding truth outside the church: that these are a 'ray of that Truth which enlightens all men' (*NA* 2). In the previous sentence when speaking of the truth and holiness found in non-Christian religions *vera* is used, whereas *Veritatis* with a capital letter is used in the phrase just cited and translated as truth with a capital 'T'. Hence, truths (in lower case) found in non-Christian religions, it is implied, are never more nor can they be, than the Truth found in Christ: 'that Truth which enlightens all men.' Therefore, it is no accident that the next sentence in *Nostra Aetate* says of the church: 'Indeed, she proclaims and must ever proclaim Christ, "the way, the truth, and the life" (John 14:6), in whom men find the fullness of religious life, and in whom God has reconciled all things to himself.' (*NA* 2; cf. 2 Cor 5:18-19)

To return to my main argument, the final context of the silence on this question is to be found in the way that negative qualifications are entered in documents apart from *Nostra Aetate* in regard to the reality of goodness and truth found outside the church and their relation to the church. This is connected to the previous point regarding fulfilment or *preparatio evangelica*. '[T]ruth' (*veritas*) is only used twice in all the conciliar documents to refer to truth outside revealed Christian Truth: once, in *Nostra Aetate* 2, regarding the Old Testament, as just noted; and the second occurrence is in *Ad Gentes* 9 – cited below. Recall that *Nostra Aetate* explicitly focuses on the positive aspects of other religions. Here, in *Ad Gentes* we find a much more nuanced appreciation of the context of truth and goodness:

> But whatever truth and grace are to be found among the nations, as a sort of secret presence of God, this [missionary] activity frees from all taint of evil and restores to Christ its maker, who overthrows the devil's domain and wards off the manifold malice of vice. And so, whatever good is found to be sown in the hearts and minds of men, or in the rites and cultures peculiar to various peoples, is not lost. More than

that, it is healed, ennobled, and perfected for the glory of God, the shame of the demon, and the bliss of men' (*AG* 9). This contextual qualification shows fulfilment proceeding via both continuity ('perfected,' 'ennobled') and discontinuity ('secret,' 'free from all taint of evil,' 'healed'). The same mix is also to be found in *Lumen Gentium* 17. This therefore indicates that other religions are a complex mixture of both truth and error, and rarely are they likely to be simply one or the other.

In the light of the above comments, I hope to have shown that it is difficult to read the conciliar documents as giving a positive answer to the question: can other religions, *per se*, in their structures, be mediators of supernatural revelation and salvific grace? While it is true that there is no explicit negative answer, there is certainly no positive answer. In the light of the last part of the analysis above it may well be the case that the documents' silences are intentional and could be read, as I would suggest, as prohibiting any unqualified positive affirmation of other religions as salvific structures, or as containing divine revelation in themselves. To be sure, this is all held, while holding at the same time, without contradiction, that supernatural saving grace is operative in other religions and that in those other religions there is much that is true, good, and holy, and much to be admired and studied and learnt from by the church.

Before moving to look at two recent papal documents that throw further light on our question, one may ask why it is that the reading I have suggested has been somewhat marginalised. Paul Knitter, the American Roman Catholic theologian, observes that: 'The majority of Catholic thinkers interpret the conciliar statements to affirm, *implicitly but clearly*, that the religions *are ways of salvation.*'[4] If Knitter is empirically correct in this judgement, then are many Catholic thinkers wrong in coming to such conclusions? The issues here are many and complex but I want to make two brief points before proceeding. First, while many Catholic theologians have indeed put forward this view, it is interesting to note that Karl Rahner, most often associated with the defence of non-Christian religions as possible means to

---

4. Paul Knitter, 'Roman Catholic Approaches to Other Religions: Developments and Tensions', *International Bulletin of Missionary Research*, 1984, 50 (my emphasis)

salvation, argues that the council texts are silent on this very point. He acknowledges that this 'essential problem' has 'been left open' and that 'Nostra Aetate gives us no information about the questions.'[5] I have been arguing that in the silence of the text, the position has not been left open in the manner Rahner suggests, but rather that it was an intentional silence given the truth of the gospel. Second, the polarised readings of the document are perhaps explicable in terms of the perceived relationship between nature and grace held by the investigating theologian. For those wanting more sharply to distinguish supernatural grace in terms of the explicit Christian revelation, the silence is seen as an intended restraint. For those wanting to relate nature and grace more closely, like Rahner in his intrinsicism, the silence is seen as an open question to be answered – affirmatively.[6]

I want to now further probe my question in the light of two papal documents: *On the Permanent Validity of the Church's Missionary Mandate (Redemptoris Missio,* 1991), and *Crossing the Threshold of Hope* (subsequently referred to as *CTH*), 1994. There are many other documents that I could draw on, and the differing status of these documents I use requires further precise clarification, but in what follows I simply want to present a number of features in Pope John Paul's thinking that helps sharpen our reading of the conciliar texts. *Crossing the Threshold of Hope* represents a running commentary on *Nostra Aetate.* With regard to the recognition in *Nostra Aetate* 2, that the church rejects 'nothing that is true and holy in these religions,' the Pope recalls the tradition of *semina Verbi* (seeds of the Word) to explain this statement, thereby locating his reading within the *preparatio evangelica* tradition. However, in so doing, he fully acknowledges that explicit elements within a religion (not the whole structure) may be used by the Holy Spirit in mediating grace to those who seek God sincerely:

5. Karl Rahner, 'On the Importance of the Non-Christian Religions for Salvation', *Theological Investigations,* vol. 18, Darton, Longman & Todd, London, 1983, 290-91
6. See Miikka Ruokanen, *The Catholic Doctrine of Non-Christian Religions according to the Second Vatican Council,* E J Brill, Leiden, 1992, 11-34, 115-20. He too isolates this as the issue underlying different approaches and offers a more restrained reading on this issue.

In another passage the council says that the Holy Spirit works effectively even outside the visible structure of the Church (cf. *Dogmatic Constitution on the Church* 13), making use of these very *semina Verbi*, that constitute a kind of common soteriological root present in all religions. (*CTH* 81) This last statement should not be read as endorsing other religions as structures *per se* for the following two reasons. First, it is in keeping with the affirming of a supernatural desire, moved by grace, implanted by God within all creation such that all women and men seek their final happiness in God. In *Sources of Renewal, The Implementation of the Second Vatican Council*, the then Cardinal Wojtyla commented on the council's depiction of Hinduism and Buddhism by saying that 'the main emphasis is laid on the search for God which for man is the core of religion, and which seems to constitute the basis of ordination between the People of God.' (130) This 'ordination' indicates the common *telos* shared by all women and men. Furthermore, when the phrase is used in *Ad Gentes* 9, it is seen in terms of 'a sort of secret presence of God' which indicates both that this may refer to the inner workings of God through conscience and the natural law (i.e. not necessarily in explicit religious structures) or to those grace-filled explicit elements that may or may not be recognised and affirmed as such by a non-Christian. Clearly, each historical case must be decided *a posteriori*. Secondly, the Pope gives precise illustrations to indicate what in a religion may act positively and what in a religion may not. To take an example, with 'primitive' and 'animistic' religions which stress ancestor worship, the Pope sees a 'kind of preparation for the Christian faith' with a direct parallel drawn between faith in ancestors and faith in the communion of saints. As the latter leads ultimately to faith in Christ, the Pope sees in this the explanation for why animists become Christians more readily than followers of the 'great' religions of the Far East (*CTH* 82). This is why he cites Hebrews 11:6, noting the possibility of 'implicit faith' in these animist traditions. Alternatively, regarding Buddhism he challenges (rightly or wrongly) its central doctrine of salvation which he claims is 'an almost exclusively negative soteriology' (*CTH* 85). And with Islam, he says of the Qur'an in regard to the Old and New Testaments that one clearly sees the process by which it completely reduces Divine Revelation. It is impossible not to note the movement away from what God said about himself, first in the Old Testament through the Prophets, and then finally in the New Testament through his Son. (*CTH* 92)

Regardless of these deeply critical judgements the Pope has no difficulty in affirming the Muslim 'religiosity' in, for example, their fidelity to prayer (*CTH* 93). This indicates that the Pope is doing no more than recognising, affirming, and celebrating those rays of truth that enlighten men and women, in mixture with error. He is not endorsing or criticising religions in general, or anyone in particular, and is clearly dialectical (in the yes/no sense) in his judgements in recognising various commonalties and also important differences. It is immaterial whether John Paul II is right or wrong in the specific judgements he makes here, but the fact that he makes them in such a manner is signifi-cant. There is never the question of any wholehearted 'yes' or 'no,' but rather always both a 'yes' and 'no', and the balance of each is in accordance with the subject matter to hand.

Finally, and perhaps somewhat definitively, *Redemptoris Missio* 29 is clear that the Pope sees the natural questing of men and women as also related to the action of the Holy Spirit within their lives. There is no clear and unambiguous nature apart from grace. In section 28 he writes: 'The Spirit, therefore, is at the very source of man's existential and religious questioning, a question which is occasioned not only by contingent situations but by the very structure of his being.' Hence, this line of thinking is in ex-plicit continuity with the conciliar documents for it acknowl-edges that grace is mediated both by the inner teleological search and also through the contingencies faced in history. This stress on history is most important. History really counts and cannot be predicted prior to its becoming. Nevertheless, this grace in creation and culture is not the fullness of sanctifying and redeeming grace found in Christ's eschatological church. Hence, all these actions of the Spirit cannot facilitate a theology of religions which affirms the various religious quests as au-thentic in themselves, apart from Christ, the Trinity, and the church. Here the Pope is keen to counter those views which seem to legitimate a reading of other religions as independent means to supernatural grace. It is worth quoting a sizeable portion of *RM* 29, for it is most important in terms of supporting my conclusions and illuminating our problem:

Thus the Spirit, who 'blows where he will' (cf. In 3:8), who 'was already at work in the world before Christ was glorified,' and who 'has filled the world … holds all things together (and) knows what is said' (Wis 1:7), leads us to broaden our vision in order to ponder his activity in every time and place. I have repeatedly called this fact to mind, and it has guided me in my meetings with a wide variety of peoples. The church's relationship with other religions is dictated by a twofold respect: 'Respect for man in his quest for answers to the deepest question of his life, and respect for the action of the Spirit in man.' Excluding any mistaken interpretation, the interreligious meeting held in Assisi was meant to confirm my conviction that 'every authentic prayer is promoted by the Holy Spirit, who is mysteriously present in every human heart'.

This is the same Spirit who was at work in the incarnation and in the life, death and resurrection of Jesus, and who is at work in the church. *He is therefore not an alternative to Christ, nor does he fill a sort of void which is sometimes suggested as existing between Christ and the Logos.* Whatever the Spirit brings about in human hearts and in the history of peoples, in cultures and religions *serves as a preparation for the gospel and can only be understood in reference to Christ,* the Word who took flesh by the power of the Spirit 'so that as perfectly human he would save all human beings and sum up all things'.

Moreover, the universal activity of the Spirit is not to be separated from his particular activity within the Body of Christ, which is the church.' (*RM* 29, my emphases)

The Pope clearly maintains a fulfilment theory as well as affirming the activity of the Holy Spirit within other religions. However, at no time is there any unqualified affirmation of the salvific value of other religions as such, while every positive statement about the other is linked to the source of all salvation, Jesus Christ, and its mediation in history, the Body of Christ, which is the church. Indeed, in an important passage, the notion of fulfilment is clear even in the context of the *sui generis* relation with

Judaism: 'The New Covenant has its roots in the Old. The time when the people of the Old Covenant will be able to see themselves *as part of the New* is, naturally, a question to be left to the Holy Spirit. We, as human beings, try only not to put obstacles in the way.' (*CTH*, 99-100, my emphasis)

In conclusion, it is to be noted that while the Pope acknowledges, as with the council, much that is good, true and holy in non-Christian religions, he is clear in keeping the council's silence intact regarding non-Christian religions as salvific structures *per se*.[7] If anything, in *Crossing the Threshold of Hope* we see John Paul II pose major and radical questions to the heart of both Buddhism and Islam. It is also clear that the grace encountered in non-Christian religions is viewed as a *preparatio evangelica*, though not in terms of a division between the grace of creation and the grace of salvation, or natural and supernatural grace, but only because within the historical church is this grace finally properly ordered toward its eschatological fulfilment. Therefore, this grace is 'not an alternative to Christ' (*RM* 29). In terms of my overall argument, I hope to have shown three things in my examination of these post-conciliar documents so far. First, the silence, indeed refusal, to acknowledge other religions, *per se*, as possibly being salvific structures, indicates that the theological positions that have been called pluralism and inclusivism are not sanctioned by the conciliar and post-conciliar documents. Second, despite this, there is no hesitation within the newly developing tradition on this question that other religions contain much that is good, true, and holy, and Christians have much to learn from them. The *a posteriori* engagement with other religions is a theological necessity for the church, in so much as the Holy Spirit is active and present in these religions. Furthermore,

---

7. This conclusion tallies with the eight thesis in the 'Notification on the book *Towards a Christian Theology of Religious Pluralism* by Father Jacques Dupuis, S.J.', CDF, 2001: 'It is therefore legitimate to maintain that the Holy Spirit accomplishes salvation in non-Christians also through those elements of truth and goodness present in the various religions; however, to hold that these religions, considered as such, are ways of salvation, has no foundation in Catholic theology, also because they contain omissions, insufficiencies and errors regarding fundamental truths about God, man and the world.' This sentence then refers to *LG*, 16; *NA* 2; *AG* 9; *RM* 55; and *Dominus Iesus* 8.

there is no ambiguity that non-Christians may be saved. Hence, there is room, beyond pluralism and inclusivism to develop a theology of religions which acknowledges that the history of religions is an important site where God may be acting.

In the remaining part of this presentation, I'd like to briefly examine the complex but decisive development to Catholic theology of religions found in *RM* with regard to the question of other religions as salvific structures.

In *Redemptoris Missio* there is an unambiguous acknowledgement that the Spirit's activity in other religions has important structural and cultural dimensions, and does not take place solely in the secret of the heart, or in some asocio-acultural location. Recall *Gaudium et Spes* 22's reticence about the manner of the Spirit's presence. Here, John Paul II is clearly developing *Gaudium et Spes*, highlighted by his close use of the documents, but prefacing his usage with an interestingly developed interpretation.

> The Spirit's presence and activity affect not only individuals but also society and history, peoples, cultures, and religions. Indeed, the Spirit is at the origin of the noble ideals and undertakings which benefit humanity on its journey through history: 'The Spirit of God, with marvellous foresight directs the course of the ages and renews the face of the earth' (*Gaudium et Spes* 26). The Risen Christ 'is now at work in human hearts through the strength of his Spirit, not only instilling a desire for the world to come but also thereby animating, purifying and reinforcing the noble aspirations which drive the human family to make its life one that is more human and to direct the whole earth to this end' (*Gaudium et Spes* 38, and see 93). (*RM* 28)

The two citations from *Gaudium et Spes* do not refer to cultures and religions, and the Pope clearly wants to push beyond any individualist reading of *Gaudium et Spes'* far-reaching affirmations. Hence *Redemptoris Missio* 28 marks an important development in affirming the implications of the Spirit's activity in structural and social terms. It refuses to see the Spirit's sanctifying activity purely in inner individualist terms. It pushes the insight regarding God's activity in the world religions to one of its tentative conclusions: these religions have structures which mediate the truth.

However, and in keeping with my previous findings, *Redemptoris Missio* then makes it absolutely clear that this recognition of the Spirit's transforming activity within other religions does not confer independent legitimacy upon other religions (in terms of their own self-understanding), because this very positive judgement is itself a Christian theological recognition (hetero-interpretation) *and* therefore relates to the reality of the Trinity within the church. This is a very important move in the argument and must be clearly distanced from any pluralist or inclusivist reading, for the reasons outlined above and in my longer study of the question.[8] In *Redemptoris Missio* there is a critique of the types of theology that have come to be advanced by Knitter or Raimundo Panikkar whereby, respectively, the Spirit is shorn of its relationship to Christ or the church, or when Jesus is seen as one of many instantiations of the eternal Logos, or when the Trinity is potentially envisaged within the economy of history as apart from, or out of relation to, the historical church and the kingdom. Of course, and rightly, no individual theologians are mentioned. To counter such positions that stray from the parameters within which discussion should take place, the encyclical first states that the presence of the Spirit is 'not an alternative to Christ, nor does he fill a sort of void which is sometimes suggested as existing between Christ and the Logos. Whatever the Spirit brings about in human hearts and in the history of peoples, in cultures and religions, serves as a preparation for the gospel and can only be understood in reference to Christ' (*RM* 29).

If we follow *Redemptoris Missio*, we see that after these important qualifications, the document turns to the ecclesiological implications of acknowledging the Holy Spirit in other religions. Hence, after this trinitarian section, *Redemptoris Missio* then relates these trinitarian themes to the church, reiterating its treatment of the 'inchoate reality' of the 'kingdom of God' present outside the church within other religions, but a reality that must nevertheless be related to the historical church:

> It is true that the inchoate reality of the kingdom can also be found beyond the confines of the church among peoples

8. See my *The Meeting of Religions and the Trinity*, T & T Clark, Edinburgh, 2000

everywhere, to the extent that they live 'gospel values' and are open to the working of the Spirit who breathes when and where he wills (cf. Jn 3:8). But it must immediately be added that this temporal dimension of the kingdom remains incomplete unless it is related to the kingdom of Christ in the church and straining toward eschatological fullness. (*RM* 20)[9]

Hence, it is clear and unambiguous that through the Spirit, God's trinitarian presence within other religions and cultures is a possibility, and one that is discerned by signs of the kingdom inchoately present within that culture. The insight of *Gaudium et Spes* 44, should also remind the church that in propounding the notion of other cultures as 'preparation for the gospel,' it is in danger of domesticating the activity of the Spirit in that religion, for the Spirit within that culture may call for an even deeper penetration, understanding and application of the truth of God's triune self-revelation entrusted to the church. That is, if the church is not attentive to the possibility of the Spirit within other religions, it will fail to be attentive to the Word of God that has been entrusted to it. In this sense, if one were to retain and utilise the category of fulfilment in a very careful sense, then it is not only the other religions that are fulfilled (and in one sense, radically transformed) such that their *preparatio* is completed through Christianity, but it is also Christianity itself that is fulfilled in receiving the gift of God that the other might bear, self-consciously or not. *Redemptoris Missio* certainly moves in this direction, even if it does not make 'fulfilment' a more dialogical and carefully qualified term.

What then are my conclusions? First, the silence of the council on other religions as salvaific structures, *per se*, was an intentional silence. It was not meant to leave the question open, as Rahner suggests, but perhaps indicates that there was no clear yes or no answer. One might say it was not answered, because the question is itself ill-conceived. Second, the post-conciliar tradition, at

---

9. Referring to the International Theological Commission, *Select Themes of Ecclesiology on the Twentieth Anniversary of the Closing of the Second Vatican Council*, Rome, 1985, ch. 10, which clearly refuses a strict identification between church and kingdom, but equally affirms an indissoluble bond between the two by virtue of Christ's presence.

least in the limited documents I have here examined, seems to support the reading I have suggested. A more exhaustive reading is required to substantiate my point. Positively, there is no question that salvation is attainable by those in other religions, and furthermore, that there are grace filled elements within those traditions. There is no hesitation in all this, so that Christians can affirm and celebrate such elements, although there is hesitation in official documents recognising that such elements, once they are incorporated and transformed within Christian practice and reflection, should be understood as part of the church's own fulfilment. Further, and negatively, so to speak, the documents refuse to say that other religions are 'paths to salvation' or 'ways' of salvation, or 'structures of salvation', because this would fail to adequately account for the error and falsity within these traditions. In one sense, this is both an *a priori* and *a posteriori* judgement as we saw in the writings of John Paul II. *A priori* because to do otherwise would logically put the church on a par with other religions as the means to salvation, and this would therefore weaken the indissoluble bond between Christ and his body, the church. *A posteriori* because to date, no other religion is trinitarian! Finally, and thirdly, my findings lead to no negative discrimination in relation to other religions. The church must be involved in serious dialogue with others, not only out of love of all women and men, but also out of love of God, for God's work and presence is clearly present within the great religious traditions of the world. For this wonderful affirmation, we are profoundly indebted to *Nostra Aetate*, a document that will be looked at retrospectively, as perhaps one of the most important documents of the council, moving the church into the new millenium – in a critical partnership with the great world faiths.

# CHAPTER TWO

# Response to Gavin D'Costa

## Daniel A. Madigan SJ

I am very grateful to have been asked to respond to Professor D'Costa's paper. His has been an important voice in the sometimes very heated, and not always sensible debate surrounding the phenomenon of religious pluralism – one of the most pressing theological questions of our time. It is not immediately clear why the person called upon to speak after the principal lecturer is called the respondent, when clearly his or her task is to pose questions. However, let me try to put some responsive questions. I approach this task not as a professional theologian, but as someone trained in Islamic studies, engaged predominantly in Muslim-Christian dialogue and in trying to interpret each of these religions for the adherents of the other.

Dr D'Costa set himself a difficult task – to prove that the silence of *Nostra Aetate* on other religions as salvific structures *per se* is not to be understood as leaving the question open, but that it should be interpreted rather as implicitly closing the discussion. He suggests that the fact that there is neither a 'yes' nor a 'no' is not to be taken as an indication that we must reflect further in order to arrive at an answer (as Rahner and others maintained). Rather the question was not answered because it is itself ill-conceived.

### Questions and answers

There are indeed problems with the question posed in this way. However, it is one we cannot evade for it is addressed to us by the very presence of the religious 'other' in our midst, and that person has a right to expect an answer from us. We are, as Levinas would say, in the literal sense of the word responsible. We must respond. And Dr D'Costa has shown in detail that the attempts to respond have continued, not only among theologians but also in documents of the magisterium, even after the rather ambiguous silence of Vatican II.[1]

The right to an answer is, of course, not necessarily the right to a positive answer, as many seem to feel. We owe the believers of other traditions a generous hearing and an honest response, rather than merely a polite one that glosses over difficulties and profound differences. Many theologies of religious pluralism are exemplary in their generosity of spirit, but in the end pay little attention to the actual reality that they are seeking to deal with. Generosity includes taking the others seriously as they are in their difference, not reducing them to reflections of myself. We are not all saying the same thing. We tend to speak of salvation as though it were a self-evident and univocal term. However, not all religions are proposing the same objective or offering the same end. Nirvana is not just heaven with an exotic name.[2]

Nor can the response we propose be a generic answer that takes no account of the variety of religious others who face and question us. This is, perhaps, one of the main difficulties we currently face in the so-called 'theology of religions.' Many are trying to find a single theology that will cover adequately all the religions. We can recall here the clarification Cardinal Ratzinger made after Jewish criticism of *Dominus Jesus*. The document had left many with the impression that the church had a one-size-fits-all approach to other religions, and Ratzinger had to underline that there is a particular relationship between Christianity and Judaism that is nothing like the relationship with any other religion.[3]

1. See also, A. Cozzi, 'Le religioni nel magistero postconciliare: problemi ermeneutici,' in *Teologia*, 28 (2002), 267-309; James L. Fredericks, 'The Catholic Church and the other religious paths: rejecting nothing that is true and holy,' in *Theological Studies*, 64.2 (June 2003) 225–254; A. Mazur 'L'insegnamento di Giovanni Paolo II sulle altre religioni.' Unpublished doctoral thesis, Gregorian University, 2003

2. Important work on this question has been done by S. Mark Heim in his two books *Salvations: truth and difference in religion* (Maryknoll: Orbis, 1995) and *The Depth of the Riches: a trinitarian theology of religious ends* (Grand Rapids: Eerdmans, 2001)

3. 'It is evident that the dialogue we Christians have with the Jews is on a different level from that with the other religions. The faith witnessed

Though Judaism clearly occupies a special place, each relationship between Christianity and another religion is particular. A Christian theology of Islam will be rather different from a Christian theology of Hinduism. Islam emerged after the Christian and Jewish traditions and, at least partly, as a critique of them. The texts sacred to Hindus and Buddhists, on the other hand, emerged long before, or at least in isolation from, those Western traditions. A single theology of religions will simply not suffice. Our response to the other must be a response to the real other. The plurality of the others calls for a plurality of responses.

John Paul II has made no secret about the fact that his experience of the religiously other has influenced his view of the question.[4] As Dr D'Costa pointed out, in *Redemptoris Missio* (28-29) the Pope has gone beyond the positions of *Nostra Aetate*, *Gaudium et Spes* and *Lumen Gentium* in explicitly affirming the active role of the Holy Spirit in human hearts and the history of peoples; and that is so not only in individuals but in the social and structural elements of cultures and religions. This recognition is a very significant step toward grappling with the issue, and it gave rise to an even further step.

In its 1997 document entitled 'Christianity and the World Religions' the International Theological Commission affirmed that 'the presence of the Holy Spirit in the religions being explicitly recognised [a reference to the advances the Pope had made in this area], it is not possible to exclude that they may as such exercise a certain salvific function, that is, despite their ambiguity, they help men achieve their ultimate end.' The Commission seems to take a different starting point from the one Dr D'Costa takes in explaining the recent magisterium's silence on the question of the religions in themselves. For him, it is because of the errors and falsity within traditions that they cannot be considered paths, ways or structures of salvation. The Commission, on the other hand, begins with the undeniable action of the Holy

in the Hebrew Bible, the Old Testament for Christians, is for us not another religion, but rather the foundation of our faith.' *Osservatore Romano*, 29 December 2000, p. 1

4. See his often-quoted speech to the Roman Curia, 22 December, 1986, published in *Osservatore Romano*, 5 January, 1987

Spirit in the religions and therefore concludes that they can indeed have a salvific function in spite of the ambiguities they may contain. Indeed, as Dr D'Costa himself puts it, 'these religions have structures which mediate the truth'.

*Can structures save us?*

When it comes to the question of the salvific value of other religious systems in themselves, I am left with a question and a comment. The question is, what does it mean exactly to speak of a religion as a salvific structure *per se*? Is it not our Christian faith that we are saved by the gracious action of God in Jesus Christ – not by a structure? This, surely, was the basis of Paul's objection to the Law. The structures, however good, of any religion, Christianity included, must not be absolutised. God alone is absolute. Even when we speak of aspects of the church as being 'of divine institution', we still recognise that these elements have been shaped by human culture and history.

Religious structures are the more or less adequate human response to the initiative of God in reaching out to us. The structures do not save us; God does. Thus the church is always called upon to purify its structures, so as to make sure that they are genuinely responding to the action of God and the demands of love, rather than expressing merely human drives and interests. Constant discernment is required if we are to avoid attributing to God what is human, and dismissing as merely human what in fact comes from God. If it is true, as Dr D'Costa says, that the question about religions as salvific structures is ill-conceived, then it is ill-conceived, at least to some extent, in all cases – Christianity included.

We Christians are inclined to speak of the 'means of salvation' as though they were things we use – tools for getting the job done. The church, we say, possesses the fullness of the means of salvation – it sounds rather too proprietorial the way some people say it – but what exactly do we mean by that? If we believe salvation is the work of God in Christ, then these 'means' must be God's instruments, not ours. God uses, for example, the sacraments – these great celebrations and re-presentations of the Christ event – to draw us more deeply into the reality of that event. How better to draw us into Christ's life than to bury us with him in baptism in the hope of resurrection, and to nourish us with him in eucharist; to assure us of the forgiveness he offered sinners, to touch and heal us as he did, to embody a faithful and fruitful love that mirrors and reveals God's love? We do not use the sacraments; God does.

However, alongside these instruments that God uses, there emerge all too often in the life of the church structures that work against the divine project of salvation. They may be once good structures gone awry, or past their time. They may be the deleterious effect of the cultures in which the gospel has become incarnate. We might claim that they are not part of the real church, but that is just playing with words. They are surely not part of the ideal church, but they really exist in the church as it actually is. There can arise situations where the actual People of God are such an obstacle to what God is trying to do, that God has to use some other means.

Perhaps, then, the question about means and structures does need to be rephrased. Instead of asking 'Is this religion a structure or vehicle of salvation?' should we not rather ask 'Are there elements in the structures of this religion that God appears to be using to save people?' Thus, there is no single, *a priori* answer to the question of how salvific other religions are. I agree with Dr D'Costa when he says this is why there cannot be a simple yes or no. We can only make an *a posteriori* judgement, based on an observation of the fruits of the Spirit and the distinguishing marks of the kingdom in the followers of that particular religion. It does not seem to me that this *a posteriori* judgement needs to be made about the whole religion, but rather about the individual elements.

In the Christian understanding, being saved means being incorporated into the divine life through the person of the fully divine, fully human one. This incorporation takes place by the gracious initiative of God, who invites a free human response. Wherever we can discern this response taking place, we are witnessing salvation – even outside the visible confines of the church. Since none of the other major traditions is based on such a concept of salvation, it would make little sense for a Christian to say that there are other ways as good as (or perhaps even better than) Christianity to arrive at the salvation we believe God is offering. Other traditions understand differently what is possible, what is promised, what is on offer. They are not simply commensurable.

*The Trinity and other religions*
The comment I wanted to make is about the trinitarian nature of other religions and what that implies for our relationship to them. This is a very important and valuable part of Dr D'Costa's paper and deserves further attention. Much of the discussion of religious pluralism focuses on what the religions mean for their members – are they salvific for them? Can they be true? Have they been superseded? However, a much more telling question is 'what do they mean for us?' Are we just sitting here sealed up and self-satisfied in our perfect religion, passing judgement on the relative value of others' religions? Or are we in a genuine relationship with the religiously other? A relationship of learning and mutual enrichment?

When we follow Pope John Paul in affirming the activity of the Spirit in the religions – including in their structures – and if we respect the tradition of the church which has long seen in other religious phenomena 'seeds of the Word', we would be splitting up the Trinity if we failed to recognise that these manifestations of Spirit and Word have their origin in the saving will and action of the Father. They are not there by mistake or accident. Therefore, there is something of the Trinity for us as Christian believers to discover in other religions, thought it will not be necessarily the same for each religion. As Dr D'Costa warns us in his paper, we risk domesticating the Spirit if we do not take seriously the Spirit's activity in other believers and their religions. The Spirit, who Jesus promised would lead us into all truth, may be calling us through the other religions to a deeper penetration into the mystery of Christ, who reveals for us the mystery of God.

So often when we use the term 'seeds of the Word' it seems a rather grudging admission that God has been at work in other religions. However, even these begrudged seeds are often thought of as wizened and shrivelled – missed opportunities, frustrated developments, fallen on rocky ground. The Indian theologian Samuel Rayan, among others, has commented that if seeds of the Word are detectable in the faith and practice of other religious communities, then surely there must be shoots and branches as well; perhaps even fruit. In the interfaith encounter the seeds are neither the dried-up reminder of a past divine initiative, nor are they a fruitfulness merely reserved for the other. They are seeds waiting to be sown in us by the God whose Word is never exhausted and who addresses us even now in the encounter with the religiously other. Not a different Word, or a new Word, but the same Word, eliciting and producing 'now thirty, now sixty, now a hundredfold' (Mk 4:8).

*Stumbling blocks*

Allow me to finish by taking up a line quoted by Dr D'Costa from *Crossing the Threshold of Hope* (99-100), where the Pope is speaking of the hope that the Jewish people, the people of the First Testament, will be brought by the Holy Spirit eventually to see themselves as part of the New Testament. He says, 'We, as human beings, try only not to put obstacles in the way.' Should not this be our watchword in all our interfaith encounter? Might it not be that the greatest obstacle to arriving at the truth of what God has done in Christ is the very community that claims to be the privileged witness to that truth? This was the burden of the Holy Father's dramatic Jubilee year *mea culpa* (perhaps better *nostra culpa, nostra maxima culpa*). We have been the stumbling block – the scandal. People have often asked themselves whether, if in the seventh century the Christian community had been a more credible witness to the revelation of God in Christ, Islam would ever have been born. Since it emerged in an environment where Christianity and Judaism were both available religious options, one can hardly avoid asking: was it the scandal of the Cross or the scandal of the church that proved the stumbling block?

To the extent that we as a Christian community live our vocation as the Body of Christ, the Word and the Spirit at work in the other religions will find answering echo in us. To the extent that we live our vocation, the Father who never ceases to labour for our salvation will be able to draw us together as sons and daughters of one family.

# CHAPTER THREE

# The Second Vatican Council and the Role of the Bible in Catholic Life

## Joseph A. Fitzmyer SJ

The Catholic Church has experienced a remarkable return to the Bible in recent decades. Catholic people, lay persons, theologians, and biblical scholars, have been devoting their time and energy not only to prayer that is biblically oriented but also to the study of the bible. This has not always been true in the centuries prior to the mid-twentieth century, especially since the time of the Reformation. Then reformers such as Martin Luther and John Calvin emphasised the study of the written Word of God in a new way and insisted on the instruction and education of the faithful in an area that had become somewhat neglected.

Part of the unfortunate heritage of the Counter-Reformation has been that Catholics tended to shy away from the bible, as if it were the Protestant book. In doing so, they lost in the post-Tridentine era much of their own Christian heritage, for sacred scripture had been a vital influence in Christian life in the patristic and medieval periods and was acquiring a new emphasis at the time of the Renaissance with its stress on *recursus ad fontes*. With those new developments in the fourteenth, fifteenth, and early sixteenth centuries, numerous Catholic scholars were in the forefront of the study of the bible and the languages in which it was originally composed, Hebrew, Aramaic, and Greek, even though the ordinary people were not well instructed in biblical teaching or the contents of the bible.

In the post-Tridentine era, when Jansenism plagued the life of the church in the seventeenth and eighteenth century, Pope Clement XI issued a Constitution, *Unigenitus Dei Filius,* which censured 101 propositions of the Frenchman, Pasquier Quesnel, one of the leaders of the Jansenist movement. The propositions were said to be 'false, captious, badly worded, offensive to pious ears, scandalous, ... blasphemous, ... and close to heresy ...'

Among the propositions were several that dealt with the bible, and from them one gains an impression of how the bible was regarded then in Catholic life. Toward the end of the seventeenth century, Quesnel had published a book entitled, *Le Nouveau Testament en francais avec des reflexions morales sur chaque verset* (1693). When he commented on the story of the Ethiopian eunuch who was returning home from a visit to Jerusalem and reading the fifty-third chapter of the prophet Isaiah in his carriage (Acts 8:28), Quesnel wrote, 'The reading of sacred scripture is for everybody.' Obviously, Quesnel thought that, if scripture itself depicts an Ethiopian eunuch reading Isaiah, then everybody should read scripture. That proposition, however, fell under papal censure in Clement XI's document. We would love to know what in it was 'offensive to pious ears' or 'close to heresy.' Another censured proposition was: 'The holy obscurity of the Word of God is not a reason for the laity to dispense themselves from the reading of it.' That was Quesnel's moral reflection on Acts 8:31, which records the Ethiopian's question, 'How can I (understand Isaiah), unless someone guides me?' Still another censured proposition was: 'Sunday ought to be kept holy by pious readings and above all by the reading of sacred scriptures. It is damnably wrong to want to withhold a Christian from such reading,' a comment on Acts 15:21, where Luke depicts James of Jerusalem saying that Moses is read every sabbath in the synagogue. I cite these censured propositions to make us aware in the twenty-first century how Catholics often lived their lives almost independently of the bible in the post-Tridentine era. Pope Clement XI obviously had good reason to censure many of the Jansenist propositions of Quesnel, but the few that deal with the reading of the bible and its role in Catholic life are still surprising and puzzling. Yet they are part of the post-Tridentine heritage, which came to an end only in the last half of the twentieth century, especially under the influence of the Second Vatican Council.

The preconciliar Catholic Church was a deeply eucharistic church, in which most of the faithful had no idea of what the 'Word of God' was all about. Catholic life was centred then on the Mass, and Catholics lived by the words of the church: occasional encyclicals of the Holy Father, pastoral instructions of their diocesan bishops, and the catechism in its various forms taught by priests and religious. Readings from the written Word of God or the bible were used in the Mass, but that was celebrated usually in Latin, and the readings were not always used for the topic of the sermon. The result was that many Catholics at that time lived abiblical or nonbiblical lives. All that changed with what happened at the Second Vatican Council, convoked by the charismatic Pope John XXIII.

Before I turn to the teaching and the effect of the Second Vatican Council itself, I must deal with the antecedents of the council, in order to put its teaching about scripture in a proper perspective. My further remarks, then, will be made under three headings: I. The antecedents of the Second Vatican Council in the area of biblical studies; II. The teaching of Vatican II on Scripture; and III. The impact of that teaching on the life of the Church.

*The antecedents of the Second Vatican Council*
*in the area of biblical studies*

I have always maintained that there never would have been a Second Vatican Council, if it were not for the 1943 encyclical of Pope Pius XII, *Divino afflante Spiritu*, 'On the Promotion of Biblical Studies'. We have all heard of that encyclical, but not many of us realise its importance. It was a 'sleeper,' because its effects did not immediately see fruition, and it took a while for Catholic people to become aware of what it was all about. The main reason for the delayed reaction to this encyclical was that it was issued in 1943, during the Second World War, when the minds of most people in the countries involved in that war were preoccupied with things other than the interpretation of the bible. With the end of World War II, there emerged in Europe what was called *la nouvelle théologie* (especially in the 1950s). It was heavily dependent on a new way of reading, studying, and interpreting scripture, in effect on the way that Pope Pius XII had recommended. This new theology and the encyclical of Pope Pius XII thus provided the background and stimulus for the council.

Before I say more about the importance of that encyclical, I

must recall two other factors, which were among the antecedents, not only of Pius XII's encyclical, but of the Second
Vatican Council itself. The first of these factors was the encyclical of Pope Leo XIII, *Providentissimus Deus*, 'On the Study of
Scripture,' issued on 18 November 1893.[1] *Divino afflante Spiritu*
of Pope Pius XII was composed to celebrate the fiftieth anniversary of Leo XIII's letter. Toward the end of the nineteenth century,
Leo XIII had to cope with the effects of the Enlightenment and its
radical approach to life and the critical interpretation of ancient
documents, such as the bible, as it sought to be rid of dogma, revelation, or anything supernatural.

Leo XIII also recognised the tremendous historical, archaeological, and scientific discoveries of the nineteenth century,
which profoundly affected the interpretation of the bible. For instance, the Rosetta Stone was discovered in the Nile Delta in
1798 by an officer of Napoleon's expedition to Egypt, but its
hieroglyphic text was not deciphered until 1822 in the work of
the Frenchman, Jean François Champollion. It took, however,
another half-century before the hieroglyphic literature of Egypt
was understood, and before the impact that that literature of ancient Israel's neighbour to the west had on the interpretation of
the Old Testament. Then one could read legal, sapiential, and
liturgical texts composed in analogous literary forms. Similarly,
the Bisitun Stone, inscribed in Elamite, Old Persian, and Assyrian,
had stood for centuries on a cliff along the old caravan-road
from Babylon to Ecbatana. Its cuneiform text was deciphered
finally about 1846 by the Englishman Henry Rawlinson, the
German Georg Grotefend, the Irishman J. Hincks, and the
Frenchman J. Oppert. As did the Rosetta Stone for Egyptian literature, so the decipherment of the Bisitun Stone opened in the
next quarter of a century the literature of the Assyrians and
Babylonians, the neighbours of ancient Israel to the east. Thus
for the first time the biblical writings of the Old Testament could
be read in the ancient context in which they had been composed.
The result of such discoveries made it clear that the bible did not
drop from heaven, and that it could no longer be interpreted

---

1. *AAS* 26 (1893-94) 279-92; *DH* 3280-94. See D. P. Béchard, *The Scripture
Documents: An Anthology of Official Catholic Teachings* (hereafter SD)
(Collegeville, MN: Liturgical Press, 2002) 37-61

without serious consideration of the similar and kindred literary forms found in this newly discovered Egyptian and Assyrian/Babylonian literature.

Because of the critical spirit of the Enlightenment, German historicism, the Babel-Bible disputes, and because of the new discoveries and the scientific advances in biology and evolution, a radically rationalist way of thinking and interpreting emerged, which Leo XIII sought to cope with in his encyclical, *Providentissimus Deus*. All of this contributed to the modernism that marked the end of the nineteenth and the beginning of the twentieth century in the Catholic Church.

The second factor that led up to *Divino afflante Spiritu* was the establishment of the Pontifical Biblical Commission by Pope Leo XIII in 1902 with his Apostolic Letter, *Vigilantiae studiique*.[2] It was an effort to further biblical scholarship and safeguard the authority of scripture against attacks of exaggerated criticism. The first word of that Letter, *Vigilantiae*, however, set the tone for the Commission's work, because it had the task of a watchdog, or of vigilantes. Among other things it had to answer questions posed to it on biblical matters; its *responsa* dealt with such matters as the Mosaic authorship of the Pentateuch (1906), the authenticity and historicity of the Johannine Gospel (1907), the historicity of Genesis 1-3 (1909). Although such *responsa* were never meant to be infallible, Pope Pius X later required of Catholics the same submission to them as to similar papally approved decrees of other Roman congregations. The result was that the Commission's *responsa* cast a dark cloud of fear and reactionary conservatism over Catholic clergy and biblical scholars in the first half of the twentieth century. Although Leo XIII acted rightly in both issuing his encyclical of 1893 and establishing the Biblical Commission in 1902, the effects of his actions, certainly unintended, were not always in the best interests of Catholic study of the bible or of Catholic life in general

These two factors, the encyclical of Leo XIII and the work of the Biblical Commission in the early years of the twentieth century, provided the background for the 1943 encyclical of Pope Pius XII. Issued on the feast of St Jerome (30 September) of that

---

2. *AAS* 35 (1902-3) 234-38; Béchard, *SD*, 62-66

year, it was a liberating force because, though he never named the method, Pius XII advocated the proper use of the historical-critical method of interpreting the bible in order to ascertain the literal sense of the inspired biblical text. In its first part, Pius XII recalled the historical background of biblical studies in the church (the encyclical of Leo XIII, various decisions of Pius X and XI, the founding of the Ecole Biblique in Jerusalem [1890], the institution of the Biblical Commission). In the second part, he built on the directives of Leo XIII, recalled the archaeological and historical discoveries, and stressed the need of recourse to the original languages of the bible, from which all future vernacular translations for use in the church henceforth were to be made. Furthermore, he insisted on the interpretation of the bible according to its literal sense, 'that the mind of the author may be made abundantly clear'. This insistence on the literal sense did not commit Catholic interpreters to any fundamentalistic literalism, but it meant that the real, religious meaning of the written Word of God had to be ascertained. Pius XII also spoke of the 'spiritual sense' of scripture, but he used that term only in its traditional meaning, i.e., the christological sense of the Old Testament. Beside the literal sense, the interpreter must explain this spiritual sense, 'provided it is clearly intended by God'. However, the 'allegorical' sense, which was used often by patristic interpreters and even recommended by Leo XIII, was not mentioned by Pius XII. He admitted, however, that 'figurative senses' of scripture might be useful in preaching, but he cautioned that such senses are 'extrinsic to it and accidental' and 'especially in these days, not free from danger'. Moreover, Pius XII clarified that 'there are but few texts whose sense has been defined by the teaching authority of the church,' and fewer still 'about which the teaching of the Holy Fathers is unanimous'. The encyclical's primary emphasis falls on interpretation of the bible according to its 'literary forms,' espousing an idea that Pope Benedict XV had rejected.

In thus setting forth guidelines for interpreting scripture, Pius XII advocated the proper use of the mode of interpretation that had been utilised for decades by both Protestant and Jewish interpreters, the so-called historical-critical method of interpretation. As a result, the interpretation of the bible by Catholic

scholars in the second half of the twentieth century began to
rival that of their Protestant and Jewish peers. It also invigorated
the study of Catholic theology, for it provided it with a solid biblical basis. This change in the mode of Catholic interpretation of
the bible was noted above all at the Second Vatican Council by
the Protestant observers, who gradually realised that Catholics
were now venerating and interpreting scripture the way that
they had been. This change led not only to the Second Vatican
Council, but also in due course to the ecumenical openness of
the Catholic Church to other Christian ecclesial communities.

*The Teaching of Vatican II on Scripture*
Although many documents of the Second Vatican Council made
use of scripture in the process of their composition, the direct
teaching of the council on scripture is found in the six chapters
of the *Dogmatic Constitution on Divine Revelation* (*Dei Verbum*,
'The Word of God').[3] After a short prologue, the Constitution
defines revelation as the way God makes known himself and his
will through creation and especially through his Son Jesus Christ
for the salvation of mankind: 'We proclaim to you the eternal life
that was with the Father and was made visible to us ...; for our
fellowship is with the Father and with his Son, Jesus Christ' (1
John 1:2-3). Revelation is, then, not simply a communication of
knowledge but a dynamic process by which the divine persons
invite human beings to enter into a relation of fellowship (chap.
1). It further teaches how that self-revelation of God is transmitted to all generations through the gospel of Christ preached by
the apostles and their successors with the help of the Holy Spirit
and is expressed in tradition and scripture, a single deposit of
the Word of God. It thus emphasises the inseparability of scripture and tradition and avoids saying that there are any revealed
truths transmitted solely by tradition (chap. 2).[4] The Constitution
likewise affirms the inspiration of scripture, teaching that it has
God as its author, who speaks through human agents and in
human fashion so that one must attend to the literary forms

3. *AAS* 58 (1966) 817-36; Béchard, *SD*, 19-33
4. See further A. Dulles, 'The Constitution on Divine Revelation in
Ecumenical Perspective,' *American Ecclesiastical Review* 154 (1966) 217-
31, esp. 220

used and to the unity of scripture in order to ascertain the intention of the inspired writers, and to realise that the sacred books teach firmly, faithfully, and without error the truth that God wanted to be recorded for the sake of our salvation (chap. 3). The Constitution then describes the Old Testament as the preparation of the salvation of all humanity in the choice of a people to whom divine promises were entrusted gradually and as a preparation for the coming of Christ, stressing that these books have meaning even for Christians (chap. 4). In chap. 5, the Constitution shows how the Word of God, which is God's power for the salvation of believers, is set forth in the writings of the New Testament, pre-eminently in the four gospels of apostolic origin, but also in other writings, all of which have to be understood properly. Finally, in chap. 6, the Constitution sets forth how scripture plays a role in the life of the church, by being along with tradition the supreme rule of faith, because in it our heavenly Father speaks to and meets his children; for this reason easy access to scripture should be available to the Christian faithful in accurate vernacular translations.

What I have just stated is a very brief *resumé* of the six chapters of this Dogmatic Constitution of the Second Vatican Council. Now I should like to home in on four particular points that make this conciliar document so important and that have contributed in a distinctive way to the role that scripture has been playing in the Catholic Church in the last forty some years.

First, in chap. 3 the Constitution stresses the venerable and traditional teaching about the inspiration of scripture, echoing the doctrine of the Council of Trent and the First Vatican Council, but it relates to that traditional teaching an important assertion about inerrancy. To explain this adequately, I must make a preliminary point about inspiration and revelation, because some Christians fail to distinguish them properly. Inspiration is not a charism that makes the writing a revelation. The Constitution had already defined revelation in chap. 1 as the self-manifestation of a personal God and the making known of the mystery of his will for the salvation of humanity. Inspiration is rather the charism by which human beings were moved by God (or by his Spirit) to record aspects or details of that divine revelation. The two ideas are not the same, or even coterminous.

It is conceivable that a whole biblical book is inspired, from the first word to the last, and yet not contain revelation. Many of the aphorisms or maxims in Ecclesiastes or in the Book of Proverbs are nuggets of human wisdom, inspired indeed, but saying nothing about the self-revealing God, his will, or his designs for human salvation. For instance, Prov 21:9 reads, 'It is better to live in a corner of the housetop than in a house shared with a contentious wife'; that is repeated in 25:24. Such a saying passes on inspired wisdom, but it is not revelation; it tells us nothing about God or his will.

When one comes to inerrancy, it has to be understood as a consequence of inspiration, but one that is not coterminous with it. It is restricted to inspired statements in the bible, and not to its questions, exclamations, or prayers. For the Constitution plainly states, 'Since everything asserted by the inspired authors or sacred writers should be regarded as asserted by the Holy Spirit, it follows that we must acknowledge the books of scripture as teaching firmly, faithfully, and without error the truth that God wished to be recorded in the sacred writings for the sake of our salvation' (11).[5] Especially noteworthy are two things, the verb 'asserted,' which is used twice, and the last phrase, 'recorded ... for the sake of our salvation.' In other words, inerrancy is the quality of all assertions in the bible that pertain to human salvation. That important phrase saves Catholic interpreters from crass fundamentalism, because it means that the charism of inerrancy does not necessarily grace every statement made with a past tense verb as if it were historically true. For this reason, the Constitution continues in 12 with a discussion about the relation of biblical truth to 'literary forms': 'Truth is differently presented and expressed in various types of historical writings, in prophetic or poetic texts, or in other modes of speech. Furthermore, the interpreter must search for what meaning the sacred writer, in his own historical situation and in accordance with the condition of his time and culture, intended to express and did in fact express with the help of literary forms that were in use during that time.' In this regard, the Constitution was reiterating what Pius XII had said less directly in *Divino afflante Spiritu* 20-21.[6]

5. Béchard, *SD*, 24
6. See Béchard, *SD*, 128-30

Second, the Constitution stresses that tradition and sacred scripture flow 'from the same divine wellspring, in a certain way come together into a single current, and tend to the same end,' because they 'form a single deposit of the Word of God, which is entrusted to the church' (10), and which is transmitted by its teaching, life, and worship. This idea is noteworthy, because, even though the council fathers knew that some theologians regarded scripture and tradition as two separate fonts or sources of revelation and did not want to condemn that view, they resolutely stated their own position about the single deposit of the Word of God.

The Constitution continues, however, with a still more important notion: 'The task of authentically interpreting the Word of God, whether in its written form or in the form of tradition, has been entrusted to the teaching office of the church, whose authority is exercised in the name of Jesus Christ. Indeed, this teaching office is not above the Word of God but serves it by teaching only what has been handed on. At the divine command and with the help of the Holy Spirit, the teaching office listens to the Word of God devoutly, guards it with dedication, and faithfully explains it. All that it proposes for belief as divinely revealed is drawn from this single deposit of faith' (10).[7] This relation of the teaching office (magisterium) to the Word of God is a novel notion, never before enunciated in the church's teaching about scripture. Note, however, the emphasis: the teaching office 'is not above the Word of God but serves it by teaching only what has been handed on.' It does not say that the teaching office is not above the written Word of God, or scripture, but that meaning of 'the Word of God' is not excluded, because in the preceding sentence 'the Word of God' is qualified, 'whether in its written form or in the form of tradition.' What the Constitution was trying to offset was the criticism sometimes heard that for Catholics the ultimate norm of belief is the magisterium. The careful formulation of paragraph 10 of *Dei Verbum* sought to correct such a view.

Third, a striking paragraph in the Constitution is found in chap. 5, when the gospels of the New Testament are discussed. I am referring to 19, which I shall quote in full:

7. Béchard, *SD*, 23

Holy Mother Church has firmly and constantly held and continues to hold that the four gospels just named, whose historicity the church affirms without hesitation, faithfully hand
on what Jesus, the Son of God, while he lived among men
and women, actually did and taught for their eternal salvation, until the day when he was taken up (cf. Acts 1:1-2). For,
after the ascension of the Lord, the apostles handed on to
their hearers what Jesus had said and done, and they did this
with that fuller understanding they now enjoyed, having
been instructed by the glorious events of Christ and taught
by the light of the Spirit of truth. In composing the four
gospels, the sacred writers selected certain of the many traditions that had been handed on either orally or already in
written form; others they summarised or explicated with an
eye to the situation of the churches. Moreover, they retained
the form and style of proclamation but always in such a fashion that they related to us an honest and true account of
Jesus. For their intention in writing was that, either from
their own memory and recollections or from the testimony of
those 'who from the beginning were eyewitnesses and minis-
ters of the Word' we might know 'the truth' concerning the
things about which we have been instructed (cf. Luke 1:2-4).[8]
Three things should be noted about this paragraph: (a) It begins
with 'Holy Mother Church,' which is derived from the title of a
document of the Biblical Commission, which by the time of the
Second Vatican Council had long since changed its image. It was
no longer the watch-dog commission of old, because from the
time of Pius XII's encyclical of 1943 it had begun to issue positive
teachings of considerable value. In 1964, during the Council itself, it published a remarkable text, 'Instruction on the Historical
Truth of the Gospels,' the opening words of which were *Sancta
Mater Ecclesia*.[9] It was remarkable, because it did not simply reit-
erate the historicity of the four gospels, but gave a very nuanced
interpretation of the gospel tradition. It turned out that the most
important word in the title was not the adjective *historica*, which
might have been one's initial expectation, but the preposition *de*,

8. Bechard, SD, 27-28
9. *Sancta Mater Ecclesia: Instructio de historica Evangeliorum veritate*,
*AAS* 56 (1964) 712-18, dated 21 April 1964.

'about, on'. The Constitution even bears a footnote (n. 35), which refers to the Biblical Commission's Instruction.

(b) Paragraph 19 begins with an affirmation of the historicity of the four gospels, which is not surprising. Some commentators on *Dei Verbum* have maintained that that affirmation resulted from one of the two factions of theologians that drew up the Constitution, the more conservative faction, which had drawn up the original schema 'On the Sources of Revelation,' which Pope John XXIII eventually rejected; it had insisted on the historicity of the gospels. Be that as it may, the end of the first sentence in the paragraph is clearly the beginning of an echo of the Biblical Commission's Instruction, which continues in the following sentences. Hence one finds a certain tension in the paragraph itself.

(c) The most important aspect of paragraph 19 is the adoption of the three stages of the gospel tradition from the Biblical Commission's Instruction. The first stage is said to represent what Jesus of Nazareth did and said while he lived on this earth and taught human beings about their salvation (= AD 1-33). The second stage represents what the apostles preached about what Jesus had done and said; that preaching, however, was carried on 'with a fuller understanding,' which they gained with the hindsight of Christ's resurrection and the illumination of the Spirit of truth (= AD 33-65). The third stage represents what the evangelists composed in their gospels, when they selected certain traditions of what had been handed on orally or in written form, summarised or synthetically combined them, and explicated them with an eye to the needs of the churches for which they were writing (= AD 65-95). This means that the Constitution clearly reckoned with the developed form of the gospel tradition which is found in the four gospels that we have inherited. Although stage three builds on stages one and two, there is more in the synoptic gospels and John than a mere stenographic report of what Jesus of Nazareth said or a cinematic record of what he did. The plus value is apostolic reflection, hindsight, and meditation on what he did and said. Fundamentalists would equate stage three with stage one, but the Constitution and the Biblical Commission's Instruction have spared Catholic interpreters that naïveté.

Fourth, the *Dogmatic Constitution on Divine Revelation* acknowledges that scripture has to be the soul of theology. In its final chapter on the role that scripture has to play in the life of the church, the Constitution recognises that both scripture and tradition are the 'permanent foundation' of sacred theology: 'The sacred scriptures contain the Word of God, and, because they are inspired, they are truly the Word of God. Therefore, let the study of the sacred page be, as it were, the soul of sacred theology' (24).[10] The Second Vatican Council referred to the same idea in its decree on Priestly Formation, *Optatam Totius* 16.[11] It has also been used in the International Theological Commission's document, *De interpretatione dogmatum*.[12] In saying that, the council fathers were echoing what Pope Leo XIII had written in *Providentissimus Deus*, 'It is most desirable and necessary that the use of the same sacred scripture should influence the discipline of theology and be, as it were, its soul' *(eiusque proprie sit anima)*.[13] It was picked up also by Pope Benedict XV in *Spiritus Paraclitus*.[14] Pope Leo XIII, however, was not the first to use the idea of scripture as the soul of theology, since it has recently been traced back to the seventeenth century, when it was used in Decree 15 of the Thirteenth General Congregation of the Society of Jesus, held at Rome in 1687: *ut anima ipsa verae theologiae*.[15] Such a role of Scripture is, of course, rightly taken for granted today, but it was not always so.

---

10. Béchard, *SD*, 29.

11. *AAS* 58 (1966) 723

12. *Gregorianum* 72 (1991) 5-37, esp. 24 (c. 1.1)

13. *AAS* 26 (1893-94) 283

14. *AAS* 12 (1920) 409

15. See *Decreta, Canones, Censurae et Praecepta Congregationum Generalium Societatis Iesu* (3 vols, Avignon: F. Seguin, 1830), 1. 262; J. W. Padberg et al., *For Matters of Greater Moment: The First Thirty Jesuit General Congregations: A Brief History and a Translation of Decrees*, (St Louis, MO: Institute of Jesuit Sources, 1994) 357. Cf. J. M. Lera, 'Sacrae paginae studium sit veluti anima Sacrae Theologiae (Notas sobre el origen y procedencia de esta frase)', *Palabra y vida: Homenaje a J. Alonso Dias en su 70 cumpleaños* (ed. A. Vargas Machuca and G. Ruiz; Madrid: UPCM, 1984) 409-22.  Also R. LaFontaine (ed.), *L'Ecriture âme de la théologie* (Collection IET 9; Brussels: Institut d'Etudes Théologiques, 1990).

Prior to the Second World War (and so, prior to Pope Pius XII's encyclical), theologians often used scripture merely as a source-book for proof-texts to support construct theses spun out almost independently of the bible. No less a theologian than Karl Rahner once sought to correct that and to establish a mutual dialogue between Catholic exegetes and dogmatic theologians. In an article entitled 'Exegese und Dogmatik,' Rahner discussed the role of both exegetes and theologians, addressing the former with the formal second plural German pronoun 'Ihr,' but using the familiar 'Du,' when he addressed his colleagues, fellow dogmatic theologians.[16] To the exegetes he said, You must remember that you too 'are Catholic theologians,' that you must pay attention to 'the Catholic principles governing the relationship between exegesis and dogmatic theology,' that you must learn to build a bridge from your investigations and interpretations to the rest of theology, and that you should have 'a more exact knowledge of scholastic theology'. Rahner, however, chided his colleagues: 'You know less about exegesis than you should. As a dogmatic theologian you rightly claim to be allowed to engage in the work of exegesis and biblical theology in your own right, and not just to accept the results of the exegetical work of the specialist ... But then you must perform the work of exegesis in the way it has to be done today and not in the way you used to do it in the good old days ... Your exegesis in dogmatic theology must be convincing also to the specialist in exegesis.'[17] Rahner wrote those words the year before the Second Vatican Council opened, but he was already aware of the idea that scripture had to be the soul of theology.

*The Impact of the Council's Teaching on the Life of the Church*
*Dei Verbum* ends with chap. 6 discussing the role of sacred scripture in the life of the church. It begins by asserting that 'the church has always venerated the divine scriptures just as she venerates the Body of the Lord, never ceasing to offer to the

16. *Stimmen der Zeit* 168 (1961) 241-62; repr. in *Schriften der Theologie* (16 vols., Einsiedeln: Benziger, 1954-84) 5 (1964) 82-111; in English, 'Exegesis and Dogmatic Theology,' *Theological Investigations* 5 (1966) 67-83, esp. 70-74
17. ibid., 77

faithful, especially in the sacred liturgy, the bread of life, received from the one table of God's Word and Christ's Body' (21). Here 'the bread of life' is given a double connotation, simultaneous sustenance from the word and the sacrament. In asserting that, the council fathers were stressing once again what had been taught in the Constitution on the Liturgy, viz., that the liturgy of the word was not just a preliminary part of the Catholic Mass, something that could really be dispensed with, but of basically equal value with the liturgy of the eucharist, because the church, as the body of Christ, is also the community of the Logos, and is fed by both his word and his flesh and blood.

Vatican II, for that reason, insisted that 'easy access to the sacred scriptures should be available to the Christian faithful,' which means that 'the church with motherly concern sees to it that suitable and accurate translations are made into various languages, especially from the original texts of the sacred books' (22). In this, the council fathers were again echoing the instruction of Pope Pius XII. They went further, however, in saying, 'If it should happen, provided the opportunity arises and the authorities of the church agree, that these translations are also produced in co-operation with the separated brethren, then all Christians will be able to use them' (22). We have seen that happen in the use of the *Revised Standard Version* of the bible in the English-speaking countries of the world.

Even though the Constitution had earlier insisted on scripture as the written Word of God, it now stresses that, along with the tradition that has grown out of it, as the church has been living through the centuries, scripture remains the supreme rule of faith. Karl Rahner explained the relation of scripture and tradition by adopting a famous Lutheran distinction, according to which scripture is the *norma normans non normata*, and tradition is the *norma normata*. That is, scripture is the norm that norms faith and all else in the church, but is itself not normed, whereas tradition is a norm of faith and life, but it is normed by scripture.[18] The reason for Rahner's adoption of this explanation was that for him, tradition

---

18. See K. Rahner, 'Scripture and Theology,' *Theological Investigations* 6 (Baltimore, MD: Helicon, 1969) 89-97, esp. 93; cf. his article, 'Bible,' *Sacramentum Mundi* (6 vols., New York: Herder and Herder, 1968-70), 1. 171-78, esp. 176-77

is nothing more than 'a legitimate unfolding of the biblical data'.[19] So understood, it is easy to understand how the twosome can be called a single deposit and the supreme rule of faith.

Again, even though the Constitution stresses that 'the interpreter of sacred scripture ... should carefully search out what the sacred writers truly intended to express and what God thought well to manifest by their words' (12), it emphasises also the need for all to realise that 'in the sacred books, the Father who is in heaven comes lovingly to meet his children and speaks with them; so great is the force and power of God's Word that it remains the sustaining life-force of the church, the strength of faith for her children, the nourishment for the soul, and the pure and lasting source of spiritual life' (21). For the revealing God still addresses Christians of the twenty-first century as he did during the millennium in which the two testaments originally came into being, and precisely through the same words (accurately translated).

What is behind these conciliar statements is the distinction often applied to scripture between what it meant to the sacred author and what it means to Christians today. The Word of God encapsulated in the words of the ancient human author revealed to him thoughts and words that were important not only to him and the ancient people for whom he recorded them, but also for believers throughout the ages who have found and still find inspiration for their lives in the Old and New Testaments. God spoke through the scriptures to his people of old, the contemporaries of the sacred writers; but he also speaks through the same inspired words to his people of today. Consequently, then, there must be a homogeneity between what it meant and what it means. What it means cannot be so diverse or different from what it meant, because then God's Word as revelation would not continue to be passed on.

It is in terms of this problem that one has to mention another document of the Biblical Commission, which appeared almost thirty years after the close of the Second Vatican Council, *The Interpretation of the Bible in the Church*, issued in 1993.[20] It is a re-

---

19. 'Scripture and Theology,' 92

20. *L'Interpretation de la Bible dans l'Eglise*, 21 September 1993 (Libreria Editrice Vaticana, 1993; cf. *Biblica* 74 [1993] 451-528)

markable document, which has been highly praised by Catholic, Jewish, and Protestant scholars. It builds on the teaching of Vatican II, taking most of the council's teaching for granted, but in one respect it goes significantly beyond the council. That has to do with what the Commission calls 'actualisation' of the written Word of God. It makes use of a French word, *actualisation*, which basically means 'modernisation' or 'making present'. Technically, it denotes the actualisation of the literal sense of the ancient human authors' inspired words, ascertained by the historical-critical method of interpretation. Those words are re-read in the light of new circumstances and applied to the contemporary situation of God's people; their message is expressed in language adapted to the present time. The Commission reckoned with the wealth of meaning of the biblical text, which gives it a value for all times and cultures. Though the biblical text is of lasting value, it sometimes is time-conditioned in its expression. There are, moreover, a dynamic unity and a complex relationship between the two Testaments, which must be acknowledged. However, one has to be wary, because the process of actualisation can run the risk of manipulating the biblical text and twisting it to a meaning that might be extrinsic to it.[21] Such actualisation often involves what is called in French *relecture*, a re-reading of the ancient text in the light of present-day events. The model for such *relecture* is found in the bible itself, when words, phrases, or themes of older written texts are used in new circumstances that add new meaning to the original sense, which was open to it. For instance, motifs from the Exodus are taken up in Deutero-Isaiah to give consolation to the people of Israel returning from the Babylonian Captivity (e.g. the motifs of Exod 15:1-8, the Song of Moses, are so used in Is 42:10-13, which calls on all to praise God as the victorious warrior; or those of Exodus 14-15, the passage through the Reed Sea, are so used in Is 43:16-17; 41:17-20); or when motifs from the plagues of Egypt and deliverance from Egypt are taken up in Wisdom 11-19.) The Commission, however, also cautions that none of these broadening aspects can be invoked to 'attribute to a biblical text whatever

21. See further R. E. Murphy, 'Reflections on Actualization of the Bible,' *BTB* 26 (1996) 79-81

meaning we like, interpreting it in a wholly subjective way,' because that would be to introduce 'alien meanings' into the text, and disrupt the homogeneity between what it meant and what it means.

Toward the end of chap. 6, *Dei Verbum* addresses priests and bishops about their obligations: 'Therefore all clerics, especially priests of Christ and others who are officially engaged as deacons and catechists in the ministry of the Word, must hold fast to the scriptures through diligent spiritual reading and careful study. This obligation must be fulfilled lest any of them become "an empty preacher of the Divine Word outwardly, who is not a listener inwardly,"[22] when they ought to be sharing with all the faithful committed to their care the abundant riches of the Divine Word, especially in the sacred liturgy. The sacred synod strongly and explicitly urges all the Christian faithful, as well, and especially religious, to learn by frequent reading of the divine scriptures "the supreme good of knowing Jesus Christ" (Phil 3:8), "For ignorance of the scriptures is ignorance of Christ"' (25), quoting St Jerome.[23]

The final paragraph of *Dei Verbum* is fittingly quoted:

In this way, therefore, let 'the Word of God speed forward and be glorified' (2 Thess 3:1), and let the treasure of revelation entrusted to the church fill human hearts ever more and more. Just as from constant participation in the eucharistic mystery the life of the church draws strength, so we may hope for a new surge of spiritual vitality from a greater veneration of the Word of God, which 'stands forever' (Is 40:8; cf. 1 Pet 1:23-25) (26).

In conclusion, then, one can see readily how far the Catholic Church has come from the days of Pope Clement XI, whose Constitution *Unigenitus Dei Filius* condemned the proposition of Pasquier Quesnel that 'the reading of sacred scripture is for everybody.' The teaching of the Second Vatican Council about scripture and its role in the life of the church sanctioned, confirmed, and at times extended the efforts of two great Popes of the nineteenth and twentieth centuries who strove to promote

22. Augustine, *Sermons* 179.1; *PL* 38.966
23. Jerome, *Comm. in Isaiam* 1.1 Prologue; *PL* 24.17

the proper veneration and study of the bible in order to enhance the spiritual lives of the Catholic faithful. *Dei Verbum* was joined at the Second Vatican Council with another important document, *Sacrosanctum Concilium* on the Divine Liturgy, and the two of them have made a tremendous difference in the life of the Catholic Church. If the church in the preconciliar days was deeply eucharistic in its life, the ecumenical council added a new player in *Dei Verbum*. Today we are all aware how much we have profited from the renewed biblical source of our Catholic lives, which received a climactic impulse in the teaching of the Second Vatican Council.

# CHAPTER FOUR

# Response to Joseph Fitzmyer

## Gerald O'Collins

When Mons Liam Bergin asked me to respond to the lecture of Fr Joseph Fitzmyer, I accepted the invitation at once and with great pleasure. This evening has provided a chance of thanking Fr Fitzmyer on my own behalf and on behalf of thousands of Catholics, Christians and others for all the wonderful ways in which he has enriched us for many years by his teaching and writing. At the start of his lecture he said: 'The Catholic Church has experienced a remarkable return to the bible in recent decades.' One of the great protagonists of that return has been Fr Fitzmyer himself – through his work as teacher, writer, editor, and member of the Pontifical Biblical Commission and other groups. Fr Fitzmyer, you have been a great scriptural benefactor of us all, and on behalf of many others, I seize this chance of saying, Thank you, thank you, thank you.

For me personally you have consistently been an immense help and inspiration. Recently I wanted to check St Paul's teaching on the effects of the Christ-event and there in your *Anchor Bible* commentary on Romans there was a beautifully clear and scholarly account of the various images the apostle used to express the saving effects of Christ's life, death, and resurrection. Your scholarship is consistently impeccable; you do not make claims without providing accurate and convincing evidence, and evidence from the primary sources – not evidence from secondary sources which may be tainted. And then the standard you and such colleagues as the late Raymond Brown have set in avoiding typographical errors has been quite extraordinary. Whenever I am correcting the proofs of a book or an article and get tired, I find courage by saying to myself: 'Joe wouldn't be careless; he would check these proofs until he dropped.'

Fr Fitzmyer, we have so much to thank you for, and not least for this evening's lecture. I was delighted to hear you recalling

the three stages in the development of the four gospels, firmly
distinguishing between inspiration and revelation, emphasising
that the truth or inerrancy of the bible is a consequence of inspiration, not identical with it, and commenting wisely on the
superb Biblical Commission document from 1993 which you
yourself helped to produce. Along the way, you offered us numerous gems, like those words from Karl Rahner to the theologians: 'your exegesis in dogmatic theology must be convincing
also to the specialist in exegesis.' Sadly, some theologians have
not yet studied the scriptures properly and not yet done their
biblical homework. Recently I found one prominent theologian
using the words of Jesus in the gospel of John as if they were
historically the *ipsissima verba* of the Lord. This misuse of the
fourth gospel allowed him to sail ahead and repeat exaggerated
claims about the human knowledge of the pre-Easter Jesus.
Obviously, Fr Fitzmyer, you still have a long way to go in convincing some theologians to follow Karl Rahner's advice and
take on board the excellent biblical scholarship you have developed and stood for.

Let me finish with two questions. First, in passing you mentioned the need for accurate translations. I wonder whether you
might like to share with us your views on current translations of
the bible: the *New American Bible*, the *New Jerusalem Bible*, the
*New Revised Standard Version*, the *Revised Standard Version*, and
so forth. What would you say about them as accurate, vernacular translations?[1] Second, apropos of the truth that God wished
to be recorded in the sacred writings for the sake of our salvation, and can look at truth as the quality of assertions which
correspond to reality. Unlike such statements as 'Who do you
say that I am?' and such exclamations of joy as 'Alleluia', statements or assertions can be true, and they are true when they correspond to reality. In saying this, I am presupposing (as you do
in your lecture) the correspondence view of truth. But what of a
view of truth as something to be done, or as truth as fidelity to

---

1. In his reply, Fr Fitzmyer endorsed the *Revised Standard Version* and
the *New American Bible* (the revision of which is still to be finished). He
expressed doubt about some renderings in the *New Revised Standard
Version* which have resulted from the translators' policy of pushing inclusive language to an extreme.

oneself and others? And what of truth as personal: for instance, in the presentation of Jesus in St John's gospel as being 'full of grace and truth' or as being 'the Truth' itself?

So, would you care to say something about current translations of the bible and what you mean by 'accurate'? And would you care to add something more about the nature of biblical truth?[2] With these two questions let me make a massive act of self-discipline and stop.

---

2. In his reply, Fr Fitzmyer simply repeated what he had said about biblical truth being the correspondence to facts which we can find in particular affirmations made in the bible. I had hoped that he would press beyond this position and add something about further themes: for instance, the divine 'truth' (*emet* in Hebrew) manifests itself in God's being utterly trustworthy and reliable; biblical 'truth' is frequently oriented towards action and transformation (e.g. 'doing the truth' and 'being set free by the truth' [John 3: 21; 8:32]); and Christ himself is 'Truth' in person. On such themes see Ch. 3 of G. O'Collins and M. Farrugia, *Catholicism. The Story of Catholic Christianity* (Oxford: Oxford University Press, 2003)

# CHAPTER FIVE

# Vatican II: The Irish Experience

## Dermot A. Lane

Most people when asked about the impact of Vatican II recall the famous remark by Archbishop John Charles McQuaid upon his return to Dublin from Rome at the end of the council in the Pro-Cathedral on 9 December:

> You may have been worried by much talk of changes to come. Allow me to reassure you. No change will worry the tranquillity of your Christian lives.[1]

The title of my paper is so vast that the most I can do in the space available is to outline a narrative of what happened since Vatican II and propose some pointers about the future.

### 1. The Event of Vatican II and its Enduring Significance

John XXlll called the council during the week of prayer for Christian Unity on 25 January, 1959 within ninety days of his election as Pope. The first session of the council opened on 11 October 1962 with 2,600 bishops in attendance. There were 200 *periti* at the first session and 480 *periti* at the final session. Around 46 observers from other churches were present at the first session and 80 at the final session. 11 laymen were at the second session and by the last session there were 52 auditors, being made up of 29 men and 33 women; it was Cardinal Suenens who suggested that the other half of humanity should be represented also at the council.

The council was called to update the church (*aggiornamento*) and to promote unity among all Christians; it opened in 1962 and closed on 8 December 1965. There were four sessions and the outcome was sixteen documents.

The meaning and significance of the Second Vatican Council in the history of the Catholic Church is a matter of intense de-

1. *Irish Times*, 10 December 1965

bate. For some Vatican II was a Council of compromise, making concessions to the minority and therefore settling little. For others the council did not teach anything new as such and therefore does not have to be taken very seriously. For still others it was a turning point in the renewal and reform of the Catholic Church. The point I want to emphasise is that this question about the meaning and intention of the Second Vatican Council is by no means an academic question. Instead it is of vital importance to the life of the church today and in the future. Whoever guards the memory of Vatican II and interprets its legacy is the one who determines the direction for the church today and tomorrow.

How then are we to interpret the historical event of the Second Vatican Council? Let me suggest some pointers. The documents surely are important in terms of what the council did and said – but, to quote Joe Komonchak, 'to give a sense of what Vatican II was as experienced and what it means as an *event*, the documents are inadequate.'[2] The teaching of Vatican II must be contextualised and that means attending carefully to the history of the council, especially the internal history of the commissions and documents. Further, the language used and the methods employed are also important pointers. Most of all the science of hermeneutics, the art of interpretation, must be applied not only to the bible but also to the documents of the church. If one examines the documents prepared for the council with the documents that were promulgated after the council one will discover what can only be described as dramatic shifts in style and substance, in language and method. The preparatory documents were neo-scholastic, authoritarian, juridical, and dogmatic in tone, whereas the promulgated texts were personalist, historical, pastoral and dialogical. If one compares the point of departure with the point of arrival one is struck immediately by a number of theological shifts. These include moves from anathema to dialogue, from the isolationism of the Catholic Church as a sub-culture to one of solidarity with the modern world, from confrontation to conversation, from uniformity to an acknowledgement of diversity, from a deductive scholastic approach to an inductive personalist

2. J. Komonchak, 'Vatican as Ecumenical Council: Yves Congar's Vision Realised', *Commonweal*, 22 November, 2002, 14

approach, from Augustinian pessimism to a more hopeful view of the present and the future.

These theological shifts in turn issued in what can be described as theological *landmarks* at Vatican II: a turn to human experience as a source of revelation,[3] a linking of faith and culture, a recognition of historical consciousness,[4] an acknowledgement of pluralism,[5] an affirmation of the existence of a hierarchy of truths in matters ecumenical,[6] a statement that the church of Christ 'subsists' in the Catholic Church as distinct from being identical with the Catholic Church, a recognition of other Christian Churches as ecclesial realities, the initiation of a new relationship between Catholicism and Judaism, and a recognition of 'elements of truth and grace' as well as 'seeds of the word' in other religions.[7]

A further pointer in any assessment of the real meaning of Vatican II is to listen to those who were present as *periti* in shaping and scripting the documents. Yves Congar OP, whose diaries on the council have recently been published, saw the council as a starting point rather than a conclusion.[8] Karl Rahner who wrote an important article on a 'Basic Theological Interpretation of the Second Vatican Council', summed up what happened at the council as a realisation by the church of itself as a worldchurch for the first time in history: in composition, in language, and in its unity with the whole world. For Rahner 'today we are for the first time living again in a period of a *caesura* like that involved in the transition from Judaeo-Christianity to Gentile Christianity'.[9]

In brief, the key to interpreting the real meaning of Vatican II is the history of what happened from the time of its announcement in January 1959 to its completion in December 1965 with the promulgation of sixteen documents. When this is done it be-

3. *DV* 14; *GS* 33
4. *GS* 4 and 5
5. *LG* 23; *DH* 1 and 2
6. *UR* 11
7. *NA* 2 and *AG* 9, 11, 15
8. See Alain Woodrow, 'Diary of an Insider', *The Tablet*, 26 October 2002, 13
9. K. Rahner, 'Basic Theological Interpretation of the Second Vatican Council', *Theological Investigations*, Vol. 20, 85

gins to emerge that Vatican II was a radical turning point in the self-understanding of the Catholic Church which included a new embrace of the modern world, the initiation of a new dialogue between the church and the world, a desire to bring about Christian unity among the churches, and an appreciation of the value of other religions.[10]

## 2. The Reception of Vatican II in Ireland

Before describing the impact of Vatican II on the church in Ireland it is necessary to say something in broad strokes about the church prior to the council. The church in Ireland in the 1940s and 1950s before Vatican II was steeped in the Catholic faith, with a high level of sacramental practise, strong devotional piety, and a real attachment to processions and pilgrimages. It was, by any standard, a conservative church, largely untouched by the enlightenment and unaffected by the developments of the modern world.

It is interesting to note, however, that in 1950 you had the foundation of *The Furrow* by Dr. J.G. McGarry of Maynooth and *Doctrine and Life*, by Father Anselm Moynihan OP in 1951. Both journals were founded to deepen the understanding of faith at that time and both were to play pivotal roles in paving the way for Vatican II and also later on in mediating the fruits of Vatican II to a wider public.

Interventions by the Irish bishops were sporadic and low key. The voices of Archbishops William Conway, John Charles McQuaid and Joseph Walsh, Bishop William Philbin and others were heard from time to time in the areas of liturgy, Marian devotion, and doctrinal matters.[11]

The first document to come out of the council was the *Constitution on the Sacred Liturgy* in December 1963 which came into effect through an Instruction in 1964. The Irish bishops issued

---

10. Of course the ongoing reception of Vatican II is also important, especially the twentieth anniversary celebration of the Council by the extraordinary Synod of Bishops in 1985 in Rome.

11. See *History of Vatican II, Vol 2: The Formation of the Council's Identity, First Period and Intercession, October 1962 to September 1963*, ed by Giuseppe Alberigo and Joseph A. Komonchak, Maryknoll, Orbis Books 1997: 110, 130, 339

a press release from Rome announcing the introduction of the
vernacular into parts of the Mass. This particular Constitution
was to have a profound effect on the Mass in Ireland: by introducing the vernacular, new translations of texts, and the re-
ordering of sanctuaries to facilitate the celebration of the Mass
facing the people.

The primary concern of the bishops in implementing Vatican
II was to bring about the changes of the council without however
disturbing the faith of the people. The one to whom this task fell
was William Conway, Archbishop of Armagh, who succeeded
Cardinal Dalton who died during the council in 1963. John
Horgan, an Irish journalist who covered the final session of the
council, recently wrote of Conway that he 'saw himself as the
manager of change *par excellence*, prodding his often reluctant
brother bishops (His Grace of Dublin excepted) out of their im-
mobilism, and at the same time restraining the enthusiasm of the
younger clergy and the laity who wanted it all and wanted it
now.'[12]

What is instructive is to observe after the council the actual
implementation of the directives in the documents. Most of the
documents resulted in the establishment of new Episcopal
Commissions. For example, the Liturgy Constitution gave rise
to a Liturgy Commission in 1964 and a Commission on Art and
Architecture in 1965. The Decree on Ecumenism issued in the establishment of the Episcopal Commission of Ecumenism 1965,
the Greenhills Conference in 1966, the Ballymacscanlon meetings from 1973 onwards, and a *Directory on Ecumenism* for
Ireland in 1976. The Decree on the Mass Media (December 1963)
resulted in the setting up of a Communications Centre in June
1965 which later developed into the Catholic Communications
Institute of Ireland in 1969 and the launch of a pastoral journal
*Intercom* in 1970. The Pastoral Constitution on the Church in the
Modern World (December 1965) saw the setting up of the Irish
Commission for Justice and Peace in 1969, the Commission for
Social Welfare in 1970, and the establishment of Trócaire in 1973.
The Decree on the Apostolate of the Laity (December 1965) gave
birth to the Irish Council for the Laity which was to be restruc-

12. John Horgan, 'Remembering How Once We Were' (A Review-arti-
cle of Louise Fuller's book), *Doctrine and Life*, April 2003, 241

tured as the Commission for the Laity in 1978. The Decree on the Missions led to the establishment of the Episcopal Commission for Missions in 1968 and the foundation of the Irish Missionary Union in 1970. The Decree on the Bishops' Pastoral Ministry gave canonical status to the Episcopal Conference in 1965. The Decree on the Ministry and Life of Priests in October 1965 resulted in 1966 in setting up of Priests' Councils in dioceses from 1967 onwards and the establishment of the National Conference of Priests of Ireland in 1975. The Decree on Christian Education (October '65) issued in the establishment of the Episcopal Catechetics Commission and the Education Commission.

Alongside these commissions a number of third level institutions came into being after Vatican II: Mater Dei Institute of Education in 1966, the Milltown Institute of Philosophy and Theology in 1968, Mount Oliver Institute of Religious Education in 1969, the Irish School of Ecumenics in 1970, and the National Centre (Institute) for Liturgy in 1970.

Also of note was the setting up of the Irish Theological Association in 1966 and the Irish Biblical Association – both of which originally received subventions from the Bishops' Conference.

Looking back at all of this activity after Vatican II, one can only be impressed and admire all that came into being. The establishment of commissions and the setting up of institutes of education gave rise to great hopes and expectations which in some instances were fulfilled and in others were frustrated. The commissions and the institutes were a mixture of genuine innovation in the Catholic Church after Vatican II and at the same time, in some instances, centres of control on developments issuing from the Council. Many of these commissions did good work and represented the church in the public domain.

One of the most serious defects, however, of this significant body of commissions is that they rarely came together as a corporate entity in the service of the gospel and the mission of the church. The absence of shared vision and an overall structure handicapped the work of the commissions. The only time they met together was at an annual reception in Maynooth, hosted by the bishops to thank the commissions for their work.

The immediate aftermath of Vatican II, however, was to be

dramatically disturbed by the publication of the encyclical *Humanae Vitae* in 1968. This encyclical created considerable controversy in the Irish church at both the pastoral and theological levels, not least because the encyclical went against the majority opinion of the expert commission set up to advise Pope Paul Vl on this most difficult question.

The real significance of *Humanae Vitae* was that it initiated an open discussion in the Irish church, not only about the morality of family planning, but also about the authority of the bishops to teach on this subject – something that was unknown and unparalleled in the past. The unquestioning obedience to the teaching authority of the bishops was breached by the debates arising out of *Humanae Vitae*. By any standards the first decade after Vatican II was a period of immense pastoral reform and theological renewal in the life of the Catholic Church.

Relationships between church and state began to change in the post-Vatican II period and this is reflected most of all in the debates surrounding contraception, abortion and divorce. Gradually there was a reluctant realisation by the bishops that Catholic morality could no longer rely as in the past on the law of the land for its enforcement. The bishops acknowledged that in the law of the state the principles peculiar to the Catholic faith could not be made binding on the people who do not adhere to that faith.[13] These debates between church and state, often acrimonious, continued right up into the new millennium.

While the church-state debates were not only inevitable and necessary, they often had a negative impact on the image of the church – putting it into a defensive mode and seeming to loose credibility in public. By focusing on these issues the false impression was also created that the only morality the church was interested in was sexual morality.

### 3. A Decade of Scandals
If the period from 1965 up to the early 1990s was stormy and controversial, the worst was yet to come in the period of 1992 to 2002. In spite of the increasing secularisation of society through the 1960s to the 1980s and the early 1990s the level of weekly at-

13. *Statement issued by the Irish Catholic Bishops Conference after their meeting in Maynooth, 14-16 June 1976.* Published in *The Furrow*, July 1976, 444

tendance of Mass, according to the European Values Study, in 1990 was found to be 85% – a figure higher than any other European country.[14]

This high rate of weekly attendance at Mass was to change very significantly in the last decade of the twentieth century. From 1992 to 2002 a series of scandals erupted in the life of the Catholic Church in Ireland. These scandals seemed to unfold progressively each year.

Between 1992 and 1994 Father Brendan Smith came to public attention, accused and charged, as a paedophile. In February 1996 a television documentary entitled 'Dear Daughter' was shown on RTÉ and this focused on an orphanage in Golden-bridge, Dublin, run by the Mercy Sisters. From April to May 1999, RTÉ put out a three-part documentary on how young people were treated in state industrial schools run by religious Orders. In May 2000 a government commission was established, headed by Judge Mary Laffoy, to enquire into child abuse in institutions of the state run by religious. In January 2002, government and CORI, after months of negotiations, reached an agreement of an upfront payment of €128 million by the religious towards a compensation fund for victims of abuse and in return the religious would be indemnified from future claims arising from child abuse in the past. In March 2002 BBC screened a documentary entitled 'Suing the Pope' about the abuse of four victims by Father Sean Fortune of Ferns Diocese. In April 2002 Micheál Martin, Minister for Health, appointed George Birmingham to advise the government on to how proceed in the Ferns Diocese. In April 2002 Bishop Brendan Commiskey resigned. At that time the Irish bishops held two emergency meetings in Maynooth to deal with the galloping crisis in regard to child sexual abuse. The bishops appointed in independent commission to be chaired by the retired Judge Gillian Hussey, on how dioceses in Ireland had dealt with the crisis of child sexual abuse. In October 2002 RTÉ broadcast a *Prime Time* programme entitled 'The Cardinal's Secrets' investigating how Cardinal

---

14. See Michael P. Hornsby-Smith and Christopher T. Whelan, 'Religious and Moral Values', *Values and Social Change in Ireland*, ed. by C.T. Whelan, Dublin, 1994, 21-22

Connell had dealt with complaints of child sexual abuse by priests in the Archdiocese of Dublin.

These events, and others not listed, provoked volumes of anger, outrage and criticism of the church. The people of Ireland were shocked, priests in parishes were demoralised, and bishops of dioceses stunned into silence.

Ordinary Catholics in the pews were scandalised for several reasons: the sacred trust placed in priests had been betrayed, a small number of priests who had committed child sexual abuse were apparently moved from parish to parish, the criminal character of child sexual abuse was ignored and not always reported to the police, the protection of the institution seems to have been more important than the pastoral care of victims, the bishops' own guidelines, drawn up in 1996, were not always followed. The inability of the institution of the church to give a credible account of its actions left a lot of people very confused.

The pastoral credibility and the moral authority of the institutional church in Ireland were shaken to their very foundations. Every month seemed to bring another revelation and as soon as one thought that it could not get any worse, a new and more shocking case emerged.

The onslaught of this series of scandals has in one sense taken us a long way from Vatican II but, in another sense, it is the context now in which Vatican II has to implemented.

4. *Challenges Facing the Catholic Church in the Light of Vatican II*
There can be little doubt in the light of the above very rough sketch of the last forty years that the Catholic Church has now arrived at a critical crossroads in Ireland. To move forward it will have to implement not just the letter but also the spirit of the Second Vatican Council and at the same time move beyond the council.

A good place to start is the *Pastoral Constitution on the Church in the Modern World* which says that 'the church has a single goal: to carry forward the work of Christ under the lead of the befriending Spirit.' To do this 'the church has always had the duty of scrutinising the signs of the times and of interpreting them in the light of the Gospel.'[15]

15. *GS* 4

I want by way of conclusion to signal some of these signs of the times calling for interpretation and action.

*a) The role of the laity.* By far the most serious neglect by the Catholic Church in Ireland since Vatican II has been the failure to activate the priesthood of the laity as outlined in the *Dogmatic Constitution on the Church, The Decree on the Apostolate of the Laity* and the Synodal Document on the *Vocation and Mission of the Laity* published in 1988.

It would, however, be inaccurate to imply that nothing has happened concerning the role of the laity in the church. In truth there have never been more lay people involved in the life of the church or indeed more lay people studying theology and religious education. The point I wish to highlight is , however, there is no pastoral plan for the laity and consequently no clear vocational pathway is available for them to participate in the pastoral ministry of the church. No formal mechanisms exist in the church for a genuine spirit of co-responsibility between priests and people or for the participation of lay people in the decision making processes of the church. It is said that if such mechanisms had existed, then the crisis provoked by child sexual abuse would have been handled differently.

If this structural defect in the life of the church is to be redressed then a programme, first of all, of adult faith formation needs to be put in place. Adult faith in Ireland is in serious trouble at present and it must be acknowledged that faith was fragile before the eruption of the crisis over sexual abuse. This combination of pressures on faith from the 1980s onwards, coupled with the scandals of child sexual abuse, has put Christian faith under severe strain in 2003. This crisis of faith is captured by the title and content of Enda McDonagh's book *Faith in Fragments*.[16] This crisis of faith is been described rather graphically by Nobel prize winner Seamus Heaney in 2002:

> I think the dwindling of faith and, secondly the clerical scandals have bewildered things ... we still are running on an unconscious that is informed by religious values, but I think my youngsters' youngsters won't have that. I think the needles are wobbling.[17]

16. E. McDonagh, *Faith in Fragments*, Dublin: Columba Press, 1996
17. Interview in the *Irish Independent Weekend*, 16 November 2002, 9

The Irish poet, Denis O'Driscoll, captures this crisis of faith in the following way in a poem entitled 'Missing God':

His grace is no longer called for before meals:
farmed fish multiply without his intercession

Miss Him when the T.V. scientist
explains the cosmos through equations
leaving our planet to resolve on its axis
aimlessly

Miss Him when we stumble on the breast lump
for the first time and an involuntary prayer
escapes our lips

Miss Him when the linen-covered
dining table holds warm bread rolls,
shining glasses of red wine.

Miss Him when, trudging past a church,
we catch a residual blast of incense.[18]

The development of a mature faith among the people of God must become a priority in the Irish church. This priority in turn must be followed up by programmes of ongoing adult religious education. What was done for school catechesis/religious education in the last thirty years now needs to be done for adult faith formation and religious education in the next thirty years.

It is only within this context of adult faith formation, ongoing adult religious education and lifelong learning that lay ministry will begin to flourish. An urgent task for church is to promote a new partnership of co-responsibility between the priesthood of the laity and the ordained priesthood – not because there is a shortage of priests but because it is demanded by virtue of one's participation in the sacraments of baptism, confirmation and membership within the eucharistic community. This relationship between lay ministry and the ordained ministry is clearly expressed by the teaching of the Second Vatican Council, in the 1985 Extraordinary Synod of Bishops in Rome, and the Synodal Document on the *Vocation and Ministry of the Laity* (1988) and in the *Catechism of the Catholic Church*, (1994).

18. Denis O'Driscoll, *Exemplary Damages*, Dublin: Anvill Press, 2002, 29-31

The US bishops in particular have highlighted the import-ance of this vision by developing a theology of what they call 'lay-ecclesial-ministry', that is a lay person who is professionally qualified in the area of ministry and entrusted with a public role in ministry by the local bishop or pastor.[19] This Vatican II vision of lay ministry is still awaiting implementation in the Catholic Church in Ireland today.

*b) Attending to a Demoralised Clergy.* The scandals in the church since 1992, and in particular the abuse of children by a small number of priests, has deeply affected the morale of diocesan and religious priests. Further, the decline in the number of vocations to the priesthood and the dwindling number of priests available for active ministry is placing additional burdens on priests today. There is increasing evidence of burnout and breakdown among far too many priests.

It is instructive to observe that all of the caring professions in Ireland have in recent times reinvented themselves in the light of social change and cultural shifts: nurses, doctors, teachers, gardaí, counsellors, and social workers have all undergone sig-nificant reconstructions in the last twenty-five years. Part of the reinvention that has taken place among the caring professions has been a sharper job specification, an outline of responsibili-ties, establishing boundaries, engaging in quality reviews, putting in place support structures, promoting annual audits of delivery, developing required in-service on an annual basis. Something similar needs to take place today regarding the priesthood in a way that respects the vocational character of priesthood and is at the same time supportive of the well-being of priests.

In particular what is known as the clerical culture needs to be put under the microscope. This particular culture has at times been far too secretive, isolationist and self-serving; it is a culture that infects the whole institutional church and is by no means confined to priests. Compared to the emerging demands within contemporary democracy for greater openness, transparency

---

19. See US Bishops, *Called and Gifted for the Third Millennium*, USCC, 1995, and the application of this vision by Cardinal Roger Mahoney in a Pastoral Letter 'As I have Done For You', *Origins*, 4 May 2000

and accountability, this particular clerical culture is no longer viable, desirable, or healthy within society or within church.

In seeking to transform this inherited clerical culture we would do well to remember how Jesus sought to critique the clerical culture of his day. Though part of the Pharisaical tradition himself, Jesus did not flinch from condemning the Pharisees and their culture for being too closed, secretive and self-serving.[20] Above all he warned those who were called to positions of leadership in the church that they must not follow the rulers of the Gentiles, but rather take on the role of being a servant.[21]

  c) *Confronting the Scandal of Child Sexual Abuse.* When it comes to addressing child sexual abuse within the institutional church it must be acknowledged that there is no quick fix solution or cheap grace available. Beware of anyone offering easy answers to this most complicated subject. A taboo plaguing the whole of society has been exposed by reference to a segment of society. No sector within society has been able to resolve this painful issue. Both church and society are in listening and learning modes at present. There is no reason why the church, which has been found to be so wanting in this area, should not be to the forefront along with the help of others in ensuring that children are safe in the present and the future, in promoting the healing of victims, in breaking the pernicious cycle of sexual abuse, and in offering pastoral care to offenders.

  If progress is to be made in confronting the scandal of sexual abuse by clergy then some of the following issues must be addressed. It is important first and foremost that the truth about sexual abuse in the church be told, the whole truth, and not just selective segments of the truth. The full truth must include reference to the responsible as well as the irresponsible actions of all the decision-makers in this area. One of the disturbing features of this scandal in the church is that in many cases so much of the truth had to be forced out of people in positions of responsibility.

  A core principle within Catholicism has been the belief that the truth will make you free. By resisting the telling of the truth the church has lost some of its own freedom to respond compas-

20. See Mt 23; Lk 11:42ff
21. Mt 20:25

sionately and creatively to this crisis. Telling the truth, the full truth, requires, among other things, that patient attention be given to *all* of the facts and that engagement in a non-polarised conversation must begin to take place between all parties.[22]

Only when we know the truth, the painful truth, about the abuse of children by priests can we begin to repair the damage done insofar as this is humanly possible. Repairing the damage entails the performance of restorative justice in relation to the victims whose lives have been destroyed sexually and psychologically. Human lives must be put back together.

Once again we come to a core value at the centre of the Catholic tradition, namely the importance of action for justice as something integral to the gospel of Jesus Christ. If the church sidesteps the issue of justice, then its teaching on justice is jeopardised.

Only when the whole truth is told and restorative justice is done can we begin to move towards a credible process of healing and forgiveness. Talk about the possibility of healing and forgiveness without attention to the truth and justice is premature and hollow. Once again a key element within the identity of Catholicism is at stake here, namely the centrality of healing and forgiveness to the mission of the church in the world.

Already there are some positive signs that the church is beginning to take significant steps. These include the setting up at a national level by the bishops of a Child Protection Office which is led by a lay director and assisited by a multidisciplined team of lay professionals. In December 2002 a dialogue was initiated between Cardinal Desmond Connell and Marie Collins and Ken Reilly – both victims of abuse by priests in Dublin – and this has led to the acceptance by Cardinal Connell of the generous offer of help and advice by Marie Collins and Ken Reilly to the church of the Dublin Diocese. Already that advice has begun to bear fruit in agreement by the diocese to renew and develop a Support Service for victims of clerical abuse. The concept of victims contributing to the resolution of this issue is a pioneering one and holds out great promise. It is also surely significant to note that Archbishop Diarmuid Martin, the newly appointed co-

22. See Patrick Hannon, 'Child Sexual Abuse: Rules for the Debate', *The Furrow*, February 2003, 67-74

adjutor to the Dublin Diocese, has already stated in his first address to the diocese his desire to work with all who have been hurt by the church. All of these developments are important steps in what will of course be a long, difficult and painful journey.

d) *The Rehabilitation of Theology.* One of the regrettable developments since the Second Vatican Council has been the gradual deterioration of the relationship that should exist between church and theology, as well as bishops and theologians. Vatican II opened up theology, giving it new life in the service of the church, and bringing it to the centre of the church's teaching mission. Part of the excitement of the council was watching how historical scholarship, biblical studies and theological ideas began to renew and reform the mission of the church in the world over a short period of four years.

Some of this new appreciation of the role of theology was reflected in the setting up by the bishops of the Irish Theological Association. In 1969 and again in 1977 the ITA argued for the introduction of theology into the national university system – TCD being the exception. These proposals for theology in the university never got off the ground for various reasons. This failure to get theology into the university sector has turned out to be a huge loss to the intellectual and theological life of the Catholic Church in Ireland. This separation of theology and church and the lack of conversation between bishops and theologians, has resulted in losses on both sides.

The church needs theology to name the mystery of God, and theology needs the community of the church to ensure it serves the faith of people. A church without a living and critical theology runs the risk of ending up surrounded by relativism or fundamentalism. Today there is more than a little evidence that both of these extremes exist alongside each other within the Irish church. A distinctive but regrettable feature of church life at present is the absence of what might be called 'middle ground thinking', with very little room left for honest disagreements and open debate in public.

Because of these developments theology needs to be rehabilitated in the life of the Catholic Church and in Irish society

*d) Invoking a New Imagination.* A common thread running through these challenges just outlined is the need for change, change in relation to the role of the laity, change in the priesthood, change in the way we must respond to the scandal of sexual abuse, change in the way we do theology. The underlying challenge facing the Catholic Church today is not one of more reason, or more argument, or more documents, though these are important; it is rather a challenge to change the paradigm out of which the church operates; it is in brief the need for a new imagination.

Changes introduced by Vatican II in terms of the new relationship between church and world, church and other churches, church and other religions, when taken together add up to a paradigm shift requiring a new imagination. John Henry Newman in the nineteenth century noted that the challenge to faith at that time was not coming from reason but from imagination. Rahner, as indicated above, saw the realisation of the church as a world church at Vatican II as a kind of rupture comparable to the shift from Jewish Christianity to Hellenistic Christianity. This shift will succeed only if the church can live out of a new imagination. The US theologian Amos Wilder pointed out in the middle 1970s that:

> When imagination fails, doctrines become ossified, witness and proclamation wooden, doxologies and litanies empty, consolation hollow and ethics legalistic.[23]

The old imaginative framework out of which the Catholic Church has operated is no longer working; it was an imaginative construction in which the church saw itself as exclusive, separate and non-historical – characteristics of a pre-Vatican II church. Impulses from the Second Vatican Council suggest that the church now understands itself as inclusive, rooted in communion 'in Christ', organically relational, and existing in solidarity with the world.

Some will be nervous about appeals to imagination because of the chequered history of imagination within philosophy. However studies on the role of imagination in philosophy and theology, especially since the time of Immanuel Kant, show that

23. Amos N. Wilder, *Theopoetics: Theology and Religious Imagination*, Philadelphia: Fortress Press, 1976, 2

we depend all the time on the exercise of the human imagination. It is imagination that enables us to understand the past and anticipate the future so that life in the present can flourish.

Let me conclude this call for a new imagination within the Catholic Church by referring to an image used by Jesus in the New Testament as he sought to reform the ways of the Pharisees:

> No one sews a piece of unshrunk cloth on an old cloak, for the patch pulls away from the cloak, and a worse tear is made. Neither is new wine put into old wine skins; otherwise, the skins burst and the wine is spilled, and the skins are destroyed; but new wine is put into fresh wine skins and so both are preserved.

All too often the new wine of Vatican II was put into old wine skins and, as we know, those old wine skins have been bursting all around us. The time has come for the church to re-imagine itself so that the new wine of Vatican II can begin to flow. If the church is to address the ethical deficit that exists in society, if it is to fill the spiritual vacuum that is all around, and if it is to transform the increasing religious apathy, then it will need to operate out of a new imagination. The shape and colour and texture of this new imaginative reconstruction would make an interesting subject for another conference.

CHAPTER SIX

# Response to Dermot Lane

## Raphael Gallagher CSsR

Writing just before the council, though for a different context, Sean O'Faolain argued: 'The priest and the writer ought to be fighting side by side, if for nothing else than the rebuttal of the vulgarity that is pouring daily into the vacuum left in the popular mind by the dying of the old traditional way of life.' The fact that instead of fighting alongside each other they were at loggerheads says much about the type of church, and indeed type of society, that prevailed in Ireland as the council was called.

The church in Ireland hoped for a different sort of council and Irish society expected a different sort of church after the council. It is worth revisiting the responses of the Irish Hierarchy and of selected professors from Maynooth in the preparation of the council. From these responses it is clear that the church (and, at the time, that certainly meant the hierarchy) foresaw a council that would complete the work of the Council of Trent and the First Vatican Council. Underlying these responses is the presupposition that the Irish church was a near perfect organisation. If only the impending council could sort out a few internal details then the church would indeed be perfect and complete. It is not only that Monsignor P. Cremin picked out servile work as a major issue to be addressed: it is his way of arguing that is telling. He is concerned that theologians and canonists are offering different views on the question to the faithful: these disputes are unedifying and confusing, and the council should settle the matter. For ever. Among the concerns expressed by the hierarchy there is one that recurs: exempt religious orders have too much freedom and they should be more firmly set under the control of the local bishop. I doubt if all the hierarchy would have agreed with the suggestion submitted by Archbishop Walshe of Tuam that the superfluity of religious houses in Ireland should be sorted out by closing them, and sending the members abroad where they could be needed and might even do some good. But the tone is shared. The church in Ireland will be perfect if the coming council completed the work of Trent with regard to the authority of the local bishop and the work of Vatican I with regard to the authority of the Pope. In rereading these submissions I get no sense that the church in Ireland saw itself allied with anyone but itself, never mind the writers in O'Faolain's plea. A possible exception could be made for the submiss on of Professor J. Newman, also from Maynooth: his is a forceful argument in favour of a better-articulated doctrinal basis for the laity in the church. Newman wanted to move from a theology that relegated laity to roles of passivity to ones where they would be active agents within the church. This submission, because of the strikingly different tone, only confirms the overall impression. The church in Ireland, on the eve of the council, was self-preoccupied. Its energy was focused on internal questions, and it was certain that it had the resources within itself to answer any outstanding questions. The council called by Pope John XXIII as an *aggiornamento* was being anticipated in Ireland as a council that would deal with the 'any other business' left over from the agendas of Trent and Vatican I.

Forty years on, the church is still self-preoccupied. But it no longer has the confidence in its own ability to answer the obvious problems. Instead of ignoring the world outside the church, as was the case at the eve of the council, it is hard to avoid the impression that the church in Ireland is now looking to judicial and civic structures to solve its problems. The society that was of no immediate interest to the church in 1960 is being appealed to, on bended knee, for help and understanding.

There is strangeness, theologically, in both positions. A church that ignores the society in which it lives is breathing on one lung; a demoralised church, whose energy is provided from outside itself, is hardly breathing at all.

Here, I believe, is part of the response to the questions posed by Dermot Lane. The council is, indeed, best seen as an event: that is, a transforming moment that can be identified as having a determinative value in how we judge history. What is the essence of the event of The Second Vatican Council? I see it in the radical restatement of the church's relationship to the secular world, and the acute relevance of the concerns of the world for the church.

This theoretic statement has critical consequences. If the church is no longer a self-standing institution, separated from and feeling superior to everything outside it, the implication is that the church is not perfect, and cannot be. This is clearly stated in the *Dogmatic Constitution on the Church, Lumen Gentium,* paragraph 8, when it talks of the holy church being always in need of purification. Purification here implies that the church, though holy, is also somehow sinful. Had we grasped that point in Ireland, we would have coped better with the tumult of recent years. It would be most begrudging to say that the church in Ireland did not try to implement the council. In many ways, the speed of the reform was extraordinary. One of the reasons for this is the fact that the power of the hierarchy was still virtually unchallenged. A doubt remains. Was the implementation, though sincere, nonetheless based on the lingering subconsciousness of a perfect church reflected in the submissions from the hierarchy and Maynooth?

The other side of a church in need of purification is the sense of a humble church that learns from wherever aspects of truth can be found. There is no hint of this in the submissions from the hierarchy and Maynooth where the talk is of dissidents being brought into line. The council was to take a different view, as can be seen from the implication of paragraph 46 of *The Church in the Modern World, Gaudium et Spes,* which urges the church to study urgent human problems in the light of the gospel and of human experience. The implementation of the council missed out on the acceptance of the formative value of human experience. Interpreting such experience is notoriously intricate, and it can be safely said that in the history of the experience of Irish Catholics two and two rarely makes four. The fibre of the Irish Catholic experience is woven with too many strands to be reduced to one simple interpretation. It was precisely this level of many strands of experience that was excluded by the prevailing view of the church as perfect and self-contained at the eve of the council. One can note residues of that mentality in the argument that, in matters that have repercussions on the other members of

society, the canon law of the church is somehow superior to the
law of the land.

What I miss most in the implementation of the council in
Ireland is a clearer recognition that the event of the council has
redefined the relationship between church and world, world
and church. This, in the final analysis, has to do with the reason
for the church's existence. Unless the central questions are the
centre of any implementation of the council, all structural reform will fail. Those central questions, for the church, centre on
Who is God? What is the meaning of salvation? Why Jesus
Christ? One cannot ignore, I admit, that some current urgent issues, as Dermot Lane acknowledged, have to be dealt with as a
matter of justice and truth. I would find it strange, however,
were the church in Ireland to become so preoccupied with immediate problems, largely of its own making, that there would
be no concentrated energy on the questions that are burning,
slow burning but nonetheless burning, in the church in Ireland.
The questions that preoccupied the church in the Ireland of 1963
were shaped by the residue of the counter-Reformation. Insofar
as these questions preoccupied society, it was on the general
presumption that the church would sort them out anyhow. The
questions for the church now are shaped by a world that has left
those counter-Reformation questions to history in the hope of
shaping a new humanity. It is not at all clear that society in
Ireland is looking to the church for the deeper resolution of these
new questions. How much different it might have been had the
council been implemented in the light of the event that it was,
rather than in the terms of the decrees it promulgated.

Instead of re-evoking O'Faolain's lament for a lost tradition I
find a better concluding image in the lines of Patrick Kavanagh
from 'Lough Derg', written in 1942 but only published eleven
years after his death (1978):

And these pilgrims of a western reason
Were not pursuing French hot miracles …
Were not led there
By priests of Maynooth or stories of Italy or Spain …
For this is the penance of the poor …
Christendom's purge. Heretical

Around the edges, the centre's hard …
And these sad people had found the key to the lock
Of God's delight in disillusionment.

Forty years after the council, the church in Ireland is certainly heretical around the edges, though I would be less sanguine about the hardness of the centre or God being found in the dis-illusionment of many Irish Catholics. A new hardness may emerge from facing up to the essential redefining of the event of the council: a church of sinners, learning from, among others, the valid experience of all that is human. Some would argue that an Irish church that ignored surrounding society in 1960 thor-oughly deserves an Irish society that in 2003 ignores the church. I do not share that view and I believe that a return to the hard core of what the council was about will prove essential to the church and beneficial to culture in Ireland. Archbishop McQuaid expressed the view, in 1961, 'that there is a notion that a univer-sity is a school in which youth is expected to think for itself'. McQuaid clearly thought such a notion to be absurd. With the council it is not only university students who began to think for themselves, and the unfinished business of implementing the council in Ireland is related to the implications of that indepen-dent thinking which has so changed both society and church in Ireland.

# CHAPTER SEVEN

# Response to Dermot Lane

## Clare McGovern

I want to thank you for a very comprehensive and informative description of our Irish church since Vatican II. You have such an easy style that you held my interest and curiosity throughout and gave me a much-needed but enjoyable trip down memory lane! I could identify with so much of what you said, even to being on many sub-committees of Commissions which seemed to go nowhere.

I, too, was immersed very early on in the fall-out from Vatican II. I came to Rome in 1968 to begin my theological studies. Rome at that time was alive with the excitement and expectation that emerged from the breath of the Spirit blowing through the church. The renewed vision of the church engendered so much joy and hope and the documents of the council had such a dynamism that, as you so rightly said, even forty years on they can give the direction for action and genuine *aggiornamento* of the church, as the People of God. Not everyone may be of the same mind on the value of these documents, some may not have even read them, but I maintain that they are indispensable for any programme of change in the church. It is true that when the teaching of the council is contextualised through knowing the internal history of these documents, one has the opportunity to follow the development of theological thought and to appreciate the fruitful tensions which arose between the old and the new structures in the writing of the documents. It is a first-hand experience of the 'promptings of the Spirit' bringing us to a fuller knowledge of the truth. 'No change' is not the language of the Spirit. As Cardinal Newman so aptly said:
 In a higher world it is otherwise,
 But, here below, to live is to change
 And to be perfect is to have changed often.

Change may take time. It calls for risk-taking and imagination. But, as a historian once said to me, history shows that it takes fifty years for the insights of a council to take root in the church. If this is so, then we have ten years to go.

I want to make one or two more specific comments and perhaps raise a question or two.

You mentioned in your talk that, after the council, the primary concern of the Irish bishops was to bring about change without, however, disturbing the faith of the people. I find this very difficult to understand. Is this the reason why we still lack a co-ordinated pastoral plan for adult faith formation in Ireland resulting in a lot of confusion, disillusionment and indifferentism on the part of the laity?

I can specifically think of the introduction of the many changes in the liturgy which were not accompanied with the necessary instruction and explanation for the people. There were so many changes made in the churches (turning altars round, removing statutes etc.) and the people did not simply know what was happening. I am not so sure that, even at this point, they fully understand and so the richness of the liturgical renewal is to some extent lost. Some efforts were made, I admit, but I think that these efforts were piecemeal, aroused very little enthusiasm and were badly attended. The need for the development of a mature adult faith still exists. It must be undertaken urgently and with some imagination and dialogue. It could be a collegial project, but adapted at local level.

You mentioned the success of catechesis at primary and secondary level in the schools over the past thirty years. Certainly a lot has been done to train and educate catechists but I am left wondering if the catechesis has really made an impact at secondary level? In many ways our young adults cannot articulate what they believe, drift into indifferentism and quite simply go their own way. I often reflect on what a theologian friend of mine said to me some years ago. His opinion was that for adult articulation of the faith (and hopefully the living out of it) our young people need some form of religious education that is assessed by examination. Would you, with your experience and insights into the training of catechists, like to comment on this opinion?

Lay-ecclesial-ministry: I rather like this description for a public role for the laity in the church. It does not smack of clericalism. It is much more suitable than the lay permanent deaconate which leaves itself open to a clerical interpretation. My question here is to ask what can be done to give women a more public role in the church? I know that recently the 'go ahead' has been given to the Irish bishops to ordain men to the lay permanent deaconate. More men in an already top-heavy male church. Is this not an obvious opportunity for the Irish church to be more pro-active and create or suggest a public role for women forty years on from Vatican II? We are talking about 50% of the people of God. Let us not wait until there are not enough men.

John Paul II, in *Christifideles Laici*, said: 'Since in our days women are taking an increasingly active share in the whole life of society, it is very important that they participate more widely in the various fields of the church's apostolate.' I used to think that perhaps permanent deaconate for women was the answer but now I am not so sure. I opt for lay-ecclesial-ministry. This is entrusted to them by the local bishop or even parish priest. Many women are professionally qualified for leadership and have the spiritual and natural gifts. When is it going to happen? Any creative ideas? I wonder how many women will we have at Vatican III? (Last session of Vatican II: Auditors: 52 – 29 men, 33 women.)

Finally I want to comment briefly on your reference to the recent scandals in the Irish church. I was avoiding this issue, perhaps really avoiding the pain, but then it might seem that I was burying my head in the sand.

Looking at the scandals enumerated, I would classify them broadly as:

Personal misdemeanours

Sexual deviations

Institutional inadequacies

Each type evokes its own level of serious consequences.

As a Sister of Mercy, I want to give my own personal reaction to the harrowing experience of seeing all of us portrayed as merciless women in the television documentaries, *Dear Daughter* and *Suffer Little Children*.

These documentaries were a complete deletion of the charism of our congregation and the cancelling out of all our years of service to children in need. Throughout this on-slaught, we had to remain voiceless and powerless and for me this was the deepest experience of radical poverty and public insignificance. I recall hearing Guttierez, the liberation theologian, once saying that the greatest poverty was not material poverty. The greatest poverty was to have no voice and to be insignificant. So, in this particular case, we could truly identify with the poor. I appreciate the need for truth and justice to emerge for any process of healing, but forgive me if I express my anxiety to know what truth and what justice? Whose truth and whose justice? However, it is best to leave all this anxiety to the providence of God.

In connection with this 'dark night' of our church, Dermot, I would love to hear further what you had in mind when you said, 'had the full implementation of the vision of Vatican II taken place, then the handling of this crisis by the institutional church might have been different.'

Once again, many thanks for your contribution which leaves me, and I am sure some others, with a sense of challenge and the enthusiasm to face the challenge. I look forward to hearing your further comments.

CHAPTER EIGHT

# Between Memory and Promise
# Sacramental Theology Since Vatican II

## Liam Bergin

The first official document to emerge from the Second Vatican Council was the Dogmatic Constitution on the Sacred Liturgy. Promulgated on 4 December 1963, *Sacrosanctum Concilium* set a context for this ecumenical council with the bold proclamation that the liturgy 'is the summit towards which the activity of the church is directed' and at the same time it is fount from which all her power flows.'[1] As the *magna charta* of the church's worship, it has inspired and guided the reform of the liturgy in the intervening period. Today, this conciliar text continues to renew, invigorate and encourage the sacramental and liturgical life of the church.

The fortieth anniversary of the publication of *Sacrosanctum Concilium* was marked by the apostolic letter *Spiritus et Sponsa* of Pope John Paul II. It calls for a 'sort of examination of conscience' of the liturgical and sacramental life of the church to see how the conciliar teaching has been received and to foster a deepening of the vision proposed by the Second Vatican Council. The purpose of this paper is to assess the contribution that the Second Vatican Council has made to sacramental theology and to project new avenues of study and research that would facilitate a fuller reception of the conciliar teaching.

## 1. The Place of Biblical Studies in Sacramental Theology

Central to the liturgical and sacramental renewal proposed by Vatican II was the rediscovery of the power of the Word of God in the life of the church. The first forty years of the twentieth century have been described as 'dark days for Catholic biblical scholarship.'[2] The initial impetus given to Catholic scriptural

1. *Sacrosanctum Concilium*, 10
2. This is the view of R. D. Witherup, 'Modern New Testament Criticism,' in J. A. Fitzmyer & R. E. Brown, eds., *New Jerome Biblical Commentary*, London 1990, II, 1142

studies during the pontificate of Leo XIII was stifled with the emergence of the modernist crisis. Significant critical scholarship did not emerge until after the encyclical *Divino Afflante Spiritu* of Pius XII in 1943. Assessing the impact of biblical theology on theological studies during this period, Emilio Rasco claimed that until after the Second Vatican Council 'the fact remains that the general outline of theological studies remained impervious [to biblical scholarship]. Professors of Scripture certainly changed their outlook within their own fields, and many professors of fundamental and dogmatic theology felt the need for change. But that change did not come. A shock was needed, and that is exactly what the council provided – Samson brought the edifice down.'[3]

According to *Dei Verbum*, Vatican II's Dogmatic Constitution on Divine Revelation, 'the study of the sacred page should be the very soul of sacred theology' (*DV* 24). The conciliar document notes that:

Sacred theology relies on the written word of God, taken together with sacred tradition, as on a permanent foundation. By this word it is most firmly strengthened and constantly rejuvenates, as it searches out, under the light of faith, the full truth stored in the mystery of Christ.[4]

In his commentary on this text, Joseph Ratzinger[5] identified three different images that describe the relationship between scripture and theology. First, a 'static notion' is employed: scripture 'taken together with sacred tradition,' functions as the 'foundation of theology'. Just as a house cannot stand without foundations, so too this image suggests, a theological construct cannot survive without resting on the rock of the sacred page. Second, an 'organic' vision is proposed: the word 'strengthens and constantly rejuvenates' theology. The 'house' of theology is not a building that has been erected once and for all, Ratzinger

3. E. Rasco, 'Biblical Theology: Its Revival and Influence on Theological Formation' in R. Latourelle, ed., *Vatican II: Assessment and Perspectives Twenty-five Years After* (1962-1987), Vol. III, 344.
4. *Dei Verbum*, 24.
5. J. Ratzinger, 'Sacred Scripture in the Life of the Church' [Commentary on *Dei Verbum*, chapter 6] in H. Vorgrimler, ed., *Commentary on the Documents of Vatican II*, vol. III, London 1969, 262-272.

notes; it stands only because theologising continues to go on as a living activity, and so the foundation is also something that is always actively founding and hence the constant starting-point for the possibility of theology's existence. Indeed, while this sentiment had already been expressed in the encyclical *Humani Generis*, Ratzinger contends that its concrete realisation was stultified by a lack of exegetical work.[6] Third, a biological figure, first suggested by Pope Leo XIII, is proffered: the study of sacred scripture is the 'soul of sacred theology'.[7]

In the dogmatic manuals employed in Catholic seminaries before Vatican II, magisterial statements provided the starting-point, while scripture and tradition offered proof-texts in the subsequent positive theological synthesis. The result of this approach, Ratzinger claims, was that themes were neither developed from the biblical perspective, nor suggested by the scriptural texts themselves. However, in the conciliar decree on priestly formation, *Optatum totius*, the procedural order of dogmatic theology is reversed:

> Biblical themes should have first place; then, the contribution of the fathers of the church is to be considered; next, the later history of dogma is to be elucidated; and, finally all aspects of the Christian mysteries and their interconnection are to be presented.[8]

Within this understanding 'the bible must first be considered and questioned on its own terms,' and 'only then can the development of tradition and dogmatic analysis take place.'[9] This understanding of the relationship between exegesis and systematic theology has since been reiterated in the document of the Pontifical Biblical Commission on the interpretation of the bible in the church.[10]

6. J. Ratzinger, 'Sacred Scripture in the Life of the Church,' 269
7. J. Wicks, *Introduction to Theological Method*, Casale Monferrato 1994, 61, n. 22, notes that the phrase has been traced to a decree issued by the thirteenth General Congregation of the Society of Jesus in 1687. It was cited by R. Cornely on the opening page of his introduction to the books of the Old Testament in 1885. From here it was taken up by *Providentissimus Deus*.
8. *Optatam totius*, 16
9. J. Ratzinger, 'Sacred Scripture in the Life of the Church,' 269
10. Commission Biblique Pontificale, *L'Interprétation de la Bible dans*

Theology is to be biblically based, developing those themes that are suggested by the inspired texts themselves. It follows that biblical studies form a crucial component of any programme of theology not just in the seminary faculties but in other divinity colleges and in programmes of adult formation and education. In the pre-conciliar period sacramental theology had generally been reduced to a commentary (or, as in many cases, a commentary on a commentary) on the *Summa*. Now, the sacred text is to be considered first. Indeed, the significant impact of biblical studies on the renewal of sacramental theology is to be found in the sections that follow.

Recently, in articulating his vision for the church of the third millennium, Pope John Paul invited all believers to contemplate the face of Christ and to meditate on him in the scriptural word.[11] Regrettably, the initial appetite for biblical renewal that followed the council in parish-based and in other similar groups appears to have waned somewhat. Nowadays a module on psychology or on self-development is likely to attract more participants than one on the synoptic gospels or on the prophets. And yet, the growing numbers who are engaged in *lectio divina* represent a new response to the conciliar hope that the Word of God would be at the very heart of the church. In the post-conciliar period new ecclesial movements have emerged and new spiritualities have taken shape. These have brought new life and renewed enthusiasm to communities that once were aging and apathetic. However, there is little doubt but that the ongoing effectiveness and continued survival of these groups will depend on the extent to which their lives are rooted in the scriptural word.

*2. The Sacramental Life of the Church in the History of Salvation*
The Council fathers set the liturgy and the sacramental life of the church within the horizon of the history of salvation, 'whose purpose is the redemption of humanity and the perfect glorific-

*l'Eglise*, Città del Vaticano 1993. English translation to be found in J. A. Fitzmyer, *The Biblical Commission's Document 'The Interpretation of the Bible in the Church': Text and Commentary*, Roma 1995.
11. *Novo Millennio Ineunte*, 23

ation of God.'[12] Building on the research of Henri de Lubac and other exponents of the *nouvelle théologie* movement of the first half of the twentieth century, the council recognised that the wonders wrought by God in the history of the people of Israel 'were but a prelude to the work of Christ Our Lord in redeeming humankind and giving perfect glory to God.'[13]

A Christian approach to the scriptures demands that both testaments are considered. As a written record of the one history of salvation, the Jewish scriptures are also part of the *norma normans* of Christian theology. In its document on the bible and christology, the Pontifical Biblical Commission called for an 'integral christology'.[14] This is achieved only when the promise and expectation of the people of Israel are given due attention as preludes to their ulterior fulfilment in the person of Jesus Christ. Placing the Christian sacraments within the context of the history of salvation demands what might well be termed an 'integral sacramentology'. This would acknowledge that the rites and ceremonies of the people of the old covenant are types and precursors of the sacraments of the people of the new covenant. Just as the Jewishness of Jesus is recognised as an indispensable key to unlocking the definitive mission of the eschatological prophet, the semitic roots of the biblical rituals constitute an essential insight into the sacramental doctrine of the church.

In recent years, for example, studies of the Jewish notion of *zikk_rôn,* or memorial, have done much to deepen the Christian understanding of memorial. When the Jewish people remembers, it does not merely recall a past event but makes it actual within the experience of the community. To read the scripture or to commemorate Passover is to unleash the power of the salvific event that is liturgically proclaimed and to insert the community that reads and celebrates into the reality of these saving actions. The insights gleaned from this semitic category have made a profound contribution to our understanding of what it means to

---

12. *Spiritus et Sponsa,* 2
13. *Sacrosanctum Concilium,* 5
14. Commission Biblique Pontificale, *Bible et christologie,* Section 1.3.3, 69-70. An English translation is to be found in J. A. Fitzmyer, *Scripture and Christology. A Statement of the Biblical Commission with a Commentary,* New York 1986.

recite a psalm or to celebrate eucharist. In both cases, the past event that is recalled is not just remembered but re-membered as it becomes effective once again for the community that celebrates it. A similar deepening of understanding has accrued to liturgical studies and to sacramental theology from other biblical categories such as *b_r_kâh* (blessing), *pesah* (Passover) and *'ôt* (prophetic action). These studies also have the advantage of deepening the Christian understanding of sacramental categories in a language that is biblically inspired and, consequently, ecumenically appropriate.

Rooting the sacramental rites of the church in the history of salvation calls for an examination of their connection to the rites of Judaism and to the religious celebrations of other religions. In the *Summa Theologica*, which is considered to present the first great treatise on sacraments in general, St Thomas Aquinas gradually unfolds and sharpens his understanding of the sacraments. Beginning from the broad Augustinian notion of a sacrament as a sign of a holy thing, *signum rei sacrae*, Thomas rejects other approaches to the sacraments that were common at the time.[15] However, not every sign of a holy thing is a sacrament: 'a sacrament is a sign of a holy thing insofar as it makes human beings holy.' Not only are the rites of the new law covered by this definition, but so too are certain rites and ceremonies of the old law. This is reinforced by Thomas' deliberate avoidance of any reference to causality at this stage. So, according to Saint Thomas, like the New Testament sacraments, circumcision is a rite that confers grace. The Christian sacraments confer grace *hic et nunc* 'by the power of the sacrament itself which it has insofar as it is an instrument of the already realised passion of Christ.'[16] The Hebrew sacraments, however, are unable to confer grace *ex opere operato* (literally 'from the work performed,' by virtue of the action itself). All grace flows from the passion of Christ. From the perspective of the Old Testament signs, the passion is an event that lies in the future towards which they point and in which they are ultimately fulfilled.[17] Yet, despite their qualitative difference as causes of sanctification, this link between the

---

15. Summa Theologica, III, Q. 60, a. 2
16. Summa Theologica, III, Q. 70, a. 4
17. Summa Theologica, III, Q. 70, a. 4

rites of the old and those of the new dispensation is significant and must play a part in the ongoing Jewish-Christian dialogue. Central to the Jewish scriptures are the notions of jubilee and sabbath. The Holy Year 2000 was celebrated as an extraordinary jubilee. From the moment when the holy door was thrown open in St Peter's basilica to the sound of the semitic *yôbél* (the trumpet made from the horn of a ram that was used to announce special events), to the appeal for the cancellation of the foreign debt of poorer nations, this Old Testament concept inspired the Christian celebration of the great 'year of favour from God'. The call to sabbath rest takes on a greater urgency as changes in socio-economic conditions have led to profound modifications of social behaviour, radically altering the character of Sunday. Underlining the continuity between the Jewish sabbath and the Christian Day of the Lord, Pope John Paul notes that 'As certain elements of the same Jewish tradition suggest, to reach the heart of the *shabbat*, of God's 'rest', we need to recognise in both the Old and the New Testament the nuptial intensity which marks the relationship between God and his people.'[18]

Inserting the sacramental rites of the church within the broader history of salvation, reminds us that grace is bestowed beyond the sacraments and beyond the visible structures and rites of the church. As can be seen from the preceding debate between Gavin D'Costa and Dan Madigan, the role of other religions in bringing about the sanctification of their adherents, while acknowledging that Jesus Christ is the unique mediator of salvation for all humanity, is a moot theological point requiring further reflection. The role that the rites and liturgies of these other religions might play in this process is an even more complex consideration and awaits further research within the christological, ecclesiological and sacramental fields.

*3. Biblical Word and Sacramental Action*
One of the fruits of the renewed dialogue between biblical and sacramental theology is the retrieval of the intrinsic link between word and action in the biblical text and in the sacramental event. Christian theology since the Reformation had been char-

18. *Dies Domini*, 12

acterised by a false dichotomy between word and sacrament. The reformers' call for a renewed emphasis on the place of the word may well have been a justified reaction against the sacramental 'inflation' of the Middle Ages. The joint study of Karl Rahner and Eberhard Jüngel[19] has demonstrated how a Catholic and Protestant approach to these sacred rites ought to emphasise their continuity with the divine grace offered in the proclamation of the good news to God's people. This is reiterated in *Dei Verbum* as it notes that 'The church has always venerated the scriptures just as she venerates the body of the Lord, since, especially in sacred liturgy, she unceasingly receives and offers to the faithful the bread of life from the table both of God's Word and of Christ's Body.'[20]

More recently, Louis Marie Chauvet reflected on the progression from one 'table' to the other:

From the table of the scriptures to the table of the sacrament, the dynamic is traditional and irreversible. Traditional in that, from the time of Emmaus, one sees the distinctively sacramental moment preceded by a scriptural moment; irreversible in that this pattern is not at all arbitrary: we never pass from the table of the sacrament to that of the scriptures.[21]

This is why the post-conciliar revision of the rites of the Catholic Church places the liturgy of the word as an indispensable, prior moment in the ritual celebration of each sacrament. It is interesting that in the Rite of Christian Initiation of Adults (RCIA) the candidates are invited to accept the gospels as they are enrolled into the order of catechumens. The new lectionaries that emerged following the council offer a broad choice of scriptural passages and, in the Sunday and weekday cycles, place a wide gamut of the biblical story before the community that celebrates the eucharist. 'In listening to the Word of God the church grows and is built, and the wonderful works of God once wrought in many different ways in the history of salvation are represented in their mystical truth through the signs of the liturgical celebration.'[22]

---

19. K. Rahner, 'What is a Sacrament?', *Theological Investigations*, vol. 14, 135-145
20. *Dei Verbum*, 21
21. L.-M. Chauvet, *Symbol and Sacrament. A Sacramental Reinterpretation of Christian Experience*, Collegeville 1995, 22.
22. *Ordo lectionum Missae*, 7

But, the progression from word to sacrament is not merely a matter of sequence. The sacraments are a 'precipitate of the scriptures'[23] and they communicate the saving mystery proclaimed in the word in a new and radical way. While both word and sacrament express and communicate the salvific power of God, there is an inherent intensity and deepening of the divine revelation and self-communication to the church as we move from ambo to altar. This inherent continuity and growing intensity as we move from word to sacrament has been highlighted by recent studies of the 'prophetic actions' found in the Old and New Testaments.[24]

The prophets of Israel proclaimed the word of God and heralded the imminent intervention of Yahweh in the lives of the covenant people.[25] Sometimes, they performed extraordinary actions that both dramatised and prolonged their verbal message in the community to which they were sent. Jeremiah, for example, proclaimed the imminent destruction of the city of Jerusalem but many of the people did not heed his message. Undeterred, however, the prophet buys an earthenware jar, carries it to the gate of the city and breaks it on the ground. As the shocked onlookers come to terms with this unwarranted waste, Jeremiah proclaims that as this pot is shattered to pieces on the ground, so too the Lord God will destroy the Holy City and scatter its inhabitants. The prophetic action was fully in line with the message that Jeremiah had already proclaimed. Having preached in vain, the prophet was now dramatically assaulting the inhabitants with the message that he had proclaimed in word, namely, that the Lord God was about to destroy the Holy City.

The Hebrew scriptures abound with many other examples of prophetic actions. Ahijah tears a new cloak into twelve pieces to proclaim that the tribes of Israel will be sundered and scattered (1 Kings 11: 29-31). Ezekiel carries his belongings from the city to herald the deportation of the people (Ez 12:7). On a positive

23. L.-M. Chauvet, *Symbol and Sacrament*, 221
24. See L. Bergin, *O Propheticum Lavacrum: Baptism as Symbolic Act of Eschatological Salvation*, Roma 1999
25. On the symbolic actions of the Old Testament prophets see S. Amsler, *Les actes des prophètes*, Genève 1985; W. Stacey, *Prophetic Drama in the Old Testament*, London 1990

note, Jeremiah shocks the community when he buys a field in the occupied Anatoth to underline his message of restoration and hope. Interesting, however, is the claim that these actions are not merely ploys to communicate a remote intervention of God. These prophetic acts – like walking naked and barefoot, the naming of a child, shaving one's head and body, buying a loincloth and then burying it to rot, tying a stone around a book and throwing it in a river, wearing a yoke of iron, remaining celibate, marrying a prostitute, foregoing traditional burial rites – anticipate a new future. By virtue of the dramatic act the very future heralded by the prophet already takes hold of the community. When Jeremiah, in obedience to the divine will, breaks the jar, the destruction of Jerusalem has already begun. The shattered jar proclaims that the walls of the city have already been breached. In other words, the action not only heralds the future intervention of God, but it actually grafts the upcoming divine judgement onto the present experience of the people.[26]

Little study has been done on the dramatic acts of Jesus.[27] Nevertheless, the signs and miracles performed by the eschatological prophet were intrinsically linked to his preaching. They proclaimed the advent of the kingdom of God in a heightened way. Actions like the gathering of the group of twelve disciples, eating with tax-collectors and sinners, the feeding of the multitude, the ascent to Jerusalem, and the cleansing of the temple are generally accepted as New Testament prophetic actions. In continuity with the symbolic gestures of the Hebrew prophets, these actions not only point to a new intervention of God, but definitively proclaim that the end-time promise of salvation is now being offered in the words and actions of Jesus of Nazareth. These provocative gestures overcame audience resistance, obliging the witnesses to reflect on their existential circumstances and to respond in a moral way. As a word embodied through the person of the prophet, the symbolic action had an enhanced impact on the community in which it was received.

26. L. Bergin, *O Propheticum Lavacrum*, 79-110
27. See H. Schürmann, 'Jesus' Words in the Light of his Actions at the Last Supper,' *Concilium* 4/10(1968) 61-67; R. Fisichella, 'Prophecy' in R. Latourelle & R. Fisichella, eds., *Dictionary of Fundamental Theology*, Middlegreen, 1994, 788-798.

Words spill into action in Jesus' proclamation of the kingdom. The actions at the Last Supper, for example, flow from
Jesus' fundamental call to serve, from his commandment to love
one's enemies and from his willingness to give his life for the
salvation of humankind. These table actions also stand firmly in
the tradition of the Old Testament prophetic acts. As such, the
gestures with the bread and wine herald the events of the passion. In this way, Holy Thursday and Good Friday can be
viewed as a single event in the divine plan of salvation: because
Jesus proffers the broken bread and the outpoured wine as saving food and drink the *via crucis* has already begun; because the
proclamation of the kingdom is to be consummated in the
bloody immolation on Golgotha, the bloodless sacrifice in the
Upper Room is truly an offer of eschatological salvation.
Consequently, the institution of the eucharist is understood as a
prophetic act where the preaching of Jesus is dramatised in gestures that anticipate his saving death. Similarly, the other six
sacraments can be rooted in specific actions which in themselves
arise from the preaching and the fundamental attitude of the
prophet from Nazareth.[28]

Since the origin of the sacramental action is intrinsically
linked to the proclaimed word, the celebration of each sacrament is rightly to be preceded by an announcement of the word.
The introduction to the rite of penance, for example, suggests
that a text of scripture be read or recited from memory either by
the priest or by the penitent in preparation for the sacrament or
as part of the celebration itself. This biblical passage is intended
to call the sinner to conversion and to confidence in God's
mercy. The scriptural text, then, inserts this particular sacramental moment within the on-going divine plan of salvation and
stirs the heart of the penitent to seek forgiveness with confidence.

---

28. Philip Rosato, *Introduzione alla teologia dei sacramenti* (1992), argues
that the seven sacraments are rooted in specific actions which in themselves arise from the preaching of Jesus: baptism in the Jordan washing
and in Jesus' proclamation of divine justice (59-68); confirmation in the
prophetic mission of hope (69-73); eucharist in the self-giving of Jesus
at the Last Supper (82-92); penance in Jesus' ministry of peace and rec-
onciliation (73-76); anointing in Jesus' ministry of compassion (76-79);
orders in Jesus' call to serve (94-99); matrimony in the fidelity of Jesus
(99-104).

A similar approach is proposed for the other sacraments. Yet, how often is this important moment omitted from the celebration of the sacrament of the sick or, indeed, from the rite of baptism of infants! This also brings the purpose and significance of the homily into focus. According to *Dei Verbum*, 'like the Christian religion itself, all the preaching of the church must be nourished and regulated by sacred scripture.'[29] Based on the scriptural page, the homily reminds the Christian community of the wonders that God has done so that, buoyed up by the good news of salvation, they will be empowered to live this message in the concrete circumstances of their own lives.

### 4. The Eschatological Dimension of Christian Worship

Christian sacraments are commemorative, demonstrative and prognostic actions: they recall the saving actions completed by the passion of Christ; they make this saving reality present in the community that celebrates; and they look forward in hope to their fulfilment in heaven. Past, present and future dimensions coalesce in the ritual action. Immediately after the eucharistic consecration, for example, we proclaim this triple mystery of faith with the words 'Christ has died (past, commemorative), Christ is risen (present, demonstrative), Christ will come again (future, prognostic).' Saint Thomas Aquinas expressed the same reality when he summarised his eucharistic theology in the antiphon 'O sacrum convivium: O holy meal, in which the body and blood of Christ is consumed, the memory of his passion is recalled (past, commemorative), the mind is filled with grace (present, demonstrative) and the pledge of future glory is given to us (future, prognostic).'

From Trent to Vatican II, the emphasis in Catholic sacramental theology was foremost on the demonstrative aspect of the ritual action, on the grace that the sacrament imparted here and now. Various reasons have been proffered for this reduction of the sacramental sign but primary among them must be a justified but extreme Catholic reaction to the Protestant denial of the power of the sacrament to cause grace *ex opere operato*. In the earlier part of the twentieth century liturgical, patristic and biblical scholars did much to redress this imbalance. While notable ad-

---

29. *Dei Verbum*, 21

vances were made in retrieving the commemorative aspect of the sacramental sign, much still needs to be done to underline the prognostic or eschatological dimension of these liturgical actions.

*Sacrosanctum Concilium* insists on the eschatological dimension of the rites of the church. Every liturgy, it states, is a foretaste of the liturgy of the heavenly Jerusalem.[30] It is interesting that this eschatological aspect of the liturgy is the leitmotif of *Spiritus et Sponsa*. 'What, indeed, is the liturgy other than the voice of the Holy Spirit and of the Bride, holy Church, crying in unison to the Lord Jesus: 'Come'? What is the liturgy other than that pure, inexhaustible source of 'living water' from which all who thirst can freely draw the gift of God?'[31] Perhaps in giving this document an overtly eschatological title, Pope John Paul II is suggesting that, forty years after the conciliar reform of the liturgy, the prognostic dimension of the Christian rites has yet to be fully appropriated by the church.

In an eschatological perspective, sacramental actions anticipate now that fullness of life that will be given at the end of time. The eucharist, for example, is understood as much as a participation in the eschatological banquet as a commemoration of the Last Supper and Calvary. Baptism is as much an entry into the presence of the glorified Lamb of the book of Revelation as it is an insertion in the death and resurrection of Christ as proclaimed in the Letter to the Romans. In fact, underscoring the eschatological dimension of the sacramental rites places them firmly within the history of salvation which awaits its ultimate fulfilment in the Second Coming of the Lord. Further, this approach accentuates the sacraments as a participation in the paschal mystery – death, resurrection, ascension and Pentecost. It is the 'whole' Christ who is encountered in these rites. The sacraments are the means by which believers are conformed to Christ who suffered and died, who lives in glory and who continues to act through the divine *Pneuma*. By baptism, for example, Christians are made partakers in the new age and so are assured that they will be taken up in the *Parousia* that is still to come.[32]

30. *Sacrosanctum Concilium*, 8
31. *Spiritus et Sponsa*, 1
32. O. Casel, *The Mystery of Christian Worship*, London 1962, 149

Approaching the sacraments from an eschatological perspective brings the church face to face with its future. Salvation has been won in Jesus Christ but awaits fulfilment in the history of each believer. Such an approach also opens the church and its members to the unknown that inevitably lurks in the tension between inauguration and fulfilment. To live solely out of memory or commemoration of the past is to stifle and limit the possibilities of the present. But, to live out of anticipation or promise of the future is to nurture and expand the horizons of the contemporary experience of the ecclesial community. Indeed, this was precisely the experience that underpinned the Second Vatican Council as, in Pope John XXIII's prophetic vision, it sought to throw the windows of the church open to the Spirit of God who comes from beyond and leads the bride into a future far beyond human possibility or reckoning. It was that Spirit that brought the church to a new understanding of itself and of its mission in the world; it was the same Spirit that brought Catholics to an appreciation of the divine presence in the hearts of men and women of other Christian communities and of other religions. It is that Spirit that we encounter yet, creating a new future and breaking down boundaries within and beyond the church. When the ecclesial community celebrates a sacrament, it unveils in the present the power of the future. The action is orientated towards the future: eschatology is not surplus to ritual memory; it is constitutive of the liturgical action. By enacting the sacramental action, the future which is signified in it is grafted into the present experience of the worshipping community.

*5. Towards a Sacramental Spirituality*
*Spiritus et Sponsa* concludes with an appeal that a 'liturgical spirituality' be developed. This spirituality should make 'people conscious that Christ is the first "liturgist" who never ceased to act in the church and in the world through the paschal mystery continuously celebrated, and who associates the church with himself, in praise of the Father, in the unity of the Holy Spirit.'[33] What are the contours that might define such a spirituality?

In 1932, Odo Casel, a Benedictine monk at the German

---

33. *Spiritus et Sponsa*, 16

Abbey of Maria Laach, published the controversial but influential work *Das christliche Kultmysterium*[34] in which he outlined his understanding of Christian life as a participation in the saving mystery of Christ through the liturgical activity of the church. This mystery is not primarily a truth beyond human reason but is, as in the Pauline scheme of things, the hidden yet communicated reality of the saving design of God. This gradual unveiling of the divine purpose finds its fulfilment in the mystery of the passion and death of the incarnate Son. According to Casel, being a Christian entails an actual sharing in these saving acts of Christ. For this purpose, the Lord has given the church the sacraments, 'the mysteries of worship,' which bring the participants into immediate contact with God. When the ecclesial community celebrates a sacrament it comes into contact with the entire saving work of Christ: 'there is neither past nor future, only present. What is past in history, the death of Christ, for example, and what is in the future of history, his *parousia*, are present in the mystery.'[35]

This notion of the sacraments as a participation in the paschal mystery was taken up and developed by *Sacrosanctum Concilium*. The sacraments, it suggests, are not just channels of grace or sanctification but moments of encounter between the celebrating community and the Glorified Lord. Sacramental grace is no longer viewed in a quantitative manner but as the unlimited self-communication of the living God who comes face to face with the church in the liturgical action.

Furthermore, 'in the perspective of *Sacrosanctum Concilium*, the liturgical life of the church acquires a cosmic and universal scope that makes a deep mark on human time and space.'[36] This is particularly evident in the council's renewed attention to various aspects of the paschal mystery as celebrated over the liturgical year. This delineating of sacred space and time has proven to be rather successful in the 'purple' seasons of Advent and Lent. Despite the weighty commercial baggage that leans on the pre-Christmas weeks, the post-conciliar church has made great

34. Published in English as O. Casel, *The Mystery of Christian Worship*, London 1962
35. O. Casel, *The Mystery of Christian Worship*, London 1962, 142
36. *Spiritus et Sponsa*, 3

strides in the celebration of this season. The same is true of Lent, particularly if the community is following the RCIA and is preparing to welcome new members at the Easter Vigil. However, it would appear that the 'white' seasons of Christmastide and Easter have fared less well. The intense expectation and preparation that precedes Christmas Day and Easter Sunday do not translate into a prolonged mystagogical reflection on the presence of the incarnate Lord or on the glory of the Risen Christ. This might well prove a worthy point of reflection for liturgists and pastors alike.

Central to any liturgical spirituality must be the conviction that everything that the Christian community says and does is 'liturgy'. The stuff of daily living from Sunday, through the week and back again to Sunday, proclaims that God saves and that God is glorified and praised whenever men and women co-operate with grace. Christian liturgy and sacraments are not isolated events through which human beings leave the secular realm of time and space in order to enter into the sacred sphere where the sanctifying grace to be conferred is grasped as a reality beyond normal experience. These ritual actions are manifestations of that holiness which already penetrates every level of secular existence. Immediately then, a liturgical spirituality calls the Christian community to sense that divine grace which is at work in the world. Sacraments, then, as they celebrate this divine presence and bring it to fulfilment, are the symbolic representations of the graced interaction with God in the lives of the participants. According to Karl Rahner, the primary locus for the renewal of the sacramental life of the church is to be found in the 'mystagogy' which opens the mystical depth of everyday experience to believers. When this happens, sacraments are truly privileged moments in the ongoing self-communication of God to humanity.[37]

Clearly the Word of God must be central. Listening to the scriptures believers come to know the divine will for them and for the world in which they live. This word spurs the hearer to action. The experience of the Old Testament prophet may be helpful here. First of all he listens, then he communicates in

---

37. K. Rahner, 'On the Theology of Worship,' *Theological Investigations*, vol. 19, 148

word and action. The listening takes place in a context: the Word of God is communicated to him in the intimacy of his relationship with the Lord Yahweh and as a member of the chosen people. A liturgical spirituality calls for a reverent listening to the Word. 'In a society that lives at an increasingly frenetic pace, often deafened by noise and confused by the ephemeral, it is vital to rediscover the value of silence.'[38] Already there is a huge increase in the numbers of people within and beyond the church who are engaging in meditation and other forms of centring prayer. 'The liturgy, with its different moments and symbols, cannot ignore silence.'[39] Furthermore, a liturgical spirituality is inherently ecclesial: it unfolds within the community of believers and deepens the divine-human dialogue that lies at the heart of the ongoing history of salvation. The whole person is dramatically involved in communicating God's message to the covenant people. Similarly, a liturgical spirituality is an integral spirituality which touches every aspect of the believer's existence. A liturgical spirituality would offer a healthy antidote to many of the new age spiritualities that are emerging today. These are inherently individualistic and private, focusing primarily on the person's inner peace and on a vertical relationship with the Other. A liturgical spirituality binds the individual to a community that worships the Lord of Life and that strengthens the horizontal bonds of communion between its members. Moreover, it commits the ecclesial community to a way of life that anticipates the new creation. Filled with the Spirit of justice and confirmed as sons and daughters of the heavenly Father, they utter a prophetic protest to the suffering and oppression that enslave the world and, by word and action, anticipate the eschaton that lies in the future with God.

A liturgical spirituality reminds the church that it lives between memory and anticipation, between *anamnesis* and *epiclesis*. As the sacramental rites recall the wonders that God has already done in the history of salvation, they also inaugurate a future in which all is made new. To gather with others in church is not just to keep the memory of Jesus alive but to encounter that oneness that marks the fullness of time. To pour baptismal water is

38. *Spiritus et Sponsa*, 13
39. *Spiritus et Sponsa*, 13

not just to re-enact the events of the Jordan and Calvary but to enter a space where the future shapes the present. To light an Easter candle is not just to remember that first dawn of resurrection but to ignite the radiance of the eternal day. To seal with oil is not just to cast out evil or to heal a wounded heart but to participate in that final victory where suffering and pain are no more. To break bread and pour wine is not just to remember the Last Supper and the passion of Christ but to experience a world where all creation is transformed by the Spirit.

The call to formulate a liturgical spirituality is firmly rooted in the documents of the Second Vatican Council. Yet, its articulation is far from complete. To live this spirituality commits the Christian community to anticipate its hope in the future, to awaken its faith in the past and to forge a present where love finds a home between memory and promise.

# CHAPTER NINE

# Road-Signs
## Reflections on the Christian Doctrine of God

### Nicholas Lash

*In the Beginning?*

At about the time that he became bishop of Hippo (that is to say: about 395 or 396) Augustine began to write his *De Doctrina Christiana*, 'On Christian teaching'. Halfway through the third of the four Books, he set it aside, and only completed the work thirty years later.

It soon acquired classic status as a handbook of Christian doctrine, a status which, with ups and downs, it sustained until the Renaissance. Abelard made much use of it, as did Aquinas; Erasmus was a great admirer. Here is how Book One begins: 'There are two things on which all interpretation of scripture depends: the process of discovering what we need to learn, and the process of presenting what we have learnt.'[1] Accordingly, his first three Books deal with 'discovery', and the fourth with 'presentation': in other words, with consideration of the kind of *rhetoric* appropriate to Christian preaching and teaching.

As to the first three Books: Augustine draws a distinction between 'things' and 'signs'. All signs, of course, are things, 'since what is not a thing does not exist,'[2] but not all things are signs. Book One is about how we should use things (including people), and Books Two and Three are about how we should interpret signs. In other words, Augustine's *De Doctrina Christiana*, this great text on Christian doctrine which sustained its classic status for over a thousand years, is about ethics, and biblical interpretation, and homiletics. It is hardly an exaggeration to say that it contains nothing that we would expect to find, today, if we went into a bookshop and asked for a handbook of Christian doctrine.

1. Augustine, *On Christian Teaching*, trans. with introduction and notes by R. P. H. Green (Oxford: Oxford University Press, 1997), I/1, p. 8
2. ibid, 1/5, p. 9

What are we to make of this? To help us get our bearings, I draw your attention to three things about Augustine's text.

*1)* In the first place, Augustine takes it for granted that Christian doctrine is a matter of biblical interpretation. Nothing surprising there, you may say. But move on nine hundred years, to thirteenth-century Paris, and the writings of Thomas Aquinas. If you set Aquinas' biblical commentaries alongside the *Summa Theologiae*, it might seem as if, in contrast to the situation in Augustine's fourth-century Africa, something very like our modern distinction between 'biblical studies' and 'systematics' is now in place.

Remember, however, that a thirteenth-century university teacher saw himself as a master craftsman with apprentices. As well as master masons and master glaziers, there were also masters of arts. And the professor of theology was a master of scripture: *Magister in sacra pagina*, a 'master of the sacred page'. In other words, even if we did not know in what high esteem someone like Aquinas held Augustine as an authority in these matters, it would be clear that, like Augustine, he understood Christian doctrine to be a matter of inculcation in the craft of biblical interpretation.

*2)* In the second place, remember that 'doctrine' means 'teaching'. But 'teaching', in English, may refer either to a process, a practice (a craft), or to the point and content of that process. 'She's been teaching me to play the clarinet'; 'What is the bible's teaching on the treatment of one's enemies?' Now, one way of highlighting the contrast between pre-modern and modern approaches to these things would be to say that pre-modern Christianity focused on the process, and modern Christianity on the content. Let's call it a shift of emphasis from *pedagogy to information*.

I do not mean that, before the modern age, people were not interested in the content. But, in a sense, they took it for granted. In a little book that I wrote some years ago on the Apostles' Creed, I used a slogan: 'What the scriptures say at length, the Creed says briefly.'[3] That is what Wittgenstein would have called a 'grammatical' remark. If you want to know what

3. Nicholas Lash, *Believing Three Ways in One God. A Reading of the Apostles' Creed* (London: SCM Press, 1992), p. 8

Christian doctrine is, read the scriptures, with your reading guided by the shape or pattern of the Creed (the articles of which Newman called 'heads and memoranda of the church's teaching').

Now the point is that everyone knows this. Augustine did not write *De Doctrina Christiana*, nor did Aquinas write the *Summa Theologiae*, in order to provide their readers with *information*. Not that they disparaged erudition but simply that, in their view, the *purpose* of Christian pedagogy lay elsewhere.

The teacher of Christian doctrine is a master craftsman; the pupil, an apprentice. What, then, is the craft-skill which the Christian teacher hopes to share? It is, in a nutshell, that aspect of holiness, or wisdom, which we call 'understanding'. I shall come back to this.

3) In the third place, Augustine, not being a modern thinker, knows that truth takes time. For a brief period in the history of Western culture (roughly, the seventeenth and eighteenth centuries) people tended to forget this. Finding all communication unreliable, all authorities untrustworthy, all received wisdom out-of-date, the surest route to truth was to work things out for oneself. The goal of intellectual endeavour was a comprehensive grasp of everything from nowhere in particular. Even today, there are still echoes of this disincarnate myth of 'complete explanation', this dream of our becoming, intellectually, 'masters of the universe'. This, notoriously, was the boast of the final paragraphs of Stephen Hawking's *Brief History of Time*, a book bought by more and read by fewer people, than any other publication of our time! (In fairness to Hawking, however, it must be admitted that, recently, he has belatedly discovered Godel's theorem and admitted that 'our search for understanding will never come to an end'[4]).

We are, I think, at last beginning to see a recovery of the recognition that, at all times, and in all places, truth is tradition-dependent. As Augustine put it in his Preface: 'Each one of us learnt our native language by habitually hearing it spoken.'[5] Each of us comes from somewhere: from some particular stock,

4. See John Cornwell, 'Hawking's quest: a search without end', *The Tablet* (27 March 2004), pp. 4-5
5. *On Christian Teaching*, Preface/9, p. 4

some tribe, some set of stories; we are the variously enriched and burdened, healed and wounded, product of some particular people; and we must help each other work out where we, and other people, are, and where to go, and how to get there.

The imagery of *travelling* pervades Augustine's text. Growth towards wisdom is a kind of 'cleansing' of the mind: 'Let us', he says, 'consider the process of cleansing as a trek, or a voyage, to our homeland.'[6] And yet, although God's wisdom is our distant home, our destiny, it has, in Christ, already come to us: 'So', says Augustine, 'although it is actually our homeland, it has also made itself the road to our homeland.'[7] The Christian doctrine of God is a doctrine both of our destiny and our direction; it constitutes the *road-signs* given to help us find the way home. Hence my title for this lecture.

So much, you might say, for preliminaries. Now, where shall we begin? I would suggest: in the beginning. And the beginning is wherever you find yourself when you ask the question: 'Where shall we begin?' I do not want to be facetious, but an awful lot of ink and energy have been wasted, in modern theology, in debates about the appropriate 'starting-point' for a Christian doctrine of God.

Shall we (for example) begin with the oneness of God, or with God's Trinity? With proof of God's existence, or announcement of God's love? With castigation of our stiff-necked pride, or with consideration of the circumstances of contemporary culture? The simple truth is that there is no one answer to such questions which is, in every respect, and from every point of view, and for every time and place and situation, 'the' correct or appropriate reply. Begin at the beginning, and the beginning is where you find yourself when you ask the question: 'Where shall we begin?'

Dante got it right. Written some fifty years after Bonaventure wrote his 'route-map', or *Itinerarium*, the greatest poem in medieval literature begins: *Nel mezzo del camin di nostra vita*, 'in the middle of the journey of our life'. (And don't forget that where Dante found himself, at the beginning, in the middle of the journey of his life, was – in a dark wood: *una selva oscura*).

6. ibid, 1/22. pp. 12-13
7. ibid, 1/23, p. 13

*A Word of Clarification*
1. The Rhetoric of Doctrine
I mentioned earlier that Augustine's fourth Book considered the kind of rhetoric appropriate to Christian teaching. 'If listeners need information', he says, 'there must be a presentation of the facts ... To clarify disputed issues there must be rational argument and deployment of evidence. But if listeners have to be moved rather than instructed, in order to make them act decisively on the knowledge that they have ... then greater powers of oratory are required.'[8]

If, as I have suggested, the notion of 'Christian doctrine' refers, in principle, to the entire process of Christian pedagogy, then it will, on one occasion or another, in this respect or that, require the service of the entire spectrum of styles of speech and writing: prescriptive and descriptive, proclamatory and contemplative, peremptory and investigative.

Moreover, if, following Newman, we were to interpret the life, language and organisation of Christianity in relation to classic accounts of the 'threefold office' of Christ – as prophet, priest, and king – we could put some shape on this by correlating the doxological and contemplative aspects of Christian teaching to the 'priestly' office, the regulative and prescriptive to the 'kingly' and – as aspects of our duty to truth's declaration – the proclamatory, investigative and descriptive aspects to the 'prophetic' office.

On this account, however, there is one problem, *internal* to the prophetic office, on which I need to comment. It concerns the relationship between the commitment of faith and the disinterestedness that scholarship requires.

## 2. *Wissenschaft als Konfession?*

This issue is sometimes discussed under the rubric of relations between 'faith' and 'reason', as if it were a problem peculiar to Christian, or at least to religious, conviction. But this, of course, is nonsense. Dangerous and most damaging nonsense, which has, for example, ensured the comprehensive marginalisation of theology in the culture of many Western European countries; but nonsense, none the less.

8. ibid, IV/14-15, p. 104

The problem of the relations between commitment and disinterestedness arises in respect of all serious pedagogy whatsoever. As such, it was discussed in a famous lecture which Max Weber delivered to the students' organisation in the University of Munich in 1919, entitled *Wissenschaft als Beruf* (usually translated as 'Science as a Vocation', but remember that *wissenschaft* connotes all kinds of serious scholarship and enquiry). Insisting that 'we are placed on the platform solely as teachers, and not as leaders', Weber sensibly insisted that 'The prophet and the demagogue do not belong on the academic platform.'[9]

In 1954, Karl Rahner addressed a group of Christian natural scientists, taking as his topic: *Wissenschaft als 'Konfession'?*, 'Science (or Scholarship) as 'Confession'?'[10] – as in 'confession of faith'. This is to take Weber's theme and put a spin on it, reminding academics of the need to invest their integrity and, indeed, identity in their work. As Rahner put it: If the academic does not devote sufficient time and attention to the fundamental questions of his being, if he does not exist by meditating, praying, meeting the demands of the moral order ... if he allows himself to be seduced by the multiplicity of his knowledge and the practical utility of his information into becoming, instead of a man, the unintelligent [clever] robot of his science, then science and the whole refining process of consolidating the scientific picture of the world becomes for the academic a curse.'[11] Demagogy has no place in the classroom (Weber was quite right); nevertheless commitment and moral seriousness are indispensable to the quest for truth. There is a sense in which all serious and responsible enquiry lives by faith.

If, then, we focus on that modest but indispensable dimension of the larger process of Christian teaching that is concerned with what Augustine called 'rational argument and deployment of evidence'; if, in other words, we concentrate on academic theology, the question still arises: what is its goal?

9. 'Max Weber, 'Science as a Vocation', *From Max Weber: Essays in Sociology*, trans. and edited H. H. Gerth and C. Wright Mills (London: Routledge and Kegan Paul, 1948). p. 149
10. Karl Rahner, 'Science as a "Confession"?', *Theological Investigations*. III, pp. 385-400
11. ibid, p. 399

Even that question, however, is not sufficiently specific. Bernard Lonergan used to distinguish between 'theology in indirect speech' and 'theology in direct speech'. Theology in indirect speech, embracing the whole range of historical, exegetical and interpretative disciplines, seeks understanding and expression of what other people thought and said and did. But what is the aim of theology in 'direct' speech?

### 3. Explanation and Understanding

One answer, widely given in the modern world, is: 'explanation'. Thus, for example, Robert Doran, in an essay on Lonergan and von Balthasar, says that: 'explanation is what systematic theology is about.'[12] I disagree.

Explanations are stories of causes and effects. Why is there a damp patch on the ceiling? Because water is dripping through from the floor above. Why is there water dripping through? Because that blasted child let the bath overflow. End of story. End of explanation. Problem solved. The world, however, is not a problem to which God is the solution.

During the seventeenth and eighteenth centuries, the word 'god' came to be used to name the ultimate explanation of the system of the world. And, when it was realised that the system of the world required no such single, overarching explanation, 'god' was dispensed with, and modern 'atheism' was born.[13]

Explanations are factors in the networks of causes and effects that constitute the world. But God (at least as Jews, and Christians, and Muslims, understand these things) is not the explanation of the world; he is the world's creator (a distinction to which I shall return).

This may be the place for a brief remark about the so-called 'proofs' of God's existence. Whatever value such exercises may or may not have, they do not form part of the Christian doctrine of God. Perhaps that bold assertion needs spelling out a little. To take Christian doctrine (as, following Augustine, I am doing in

12. Robert Doran, 'Lonergan and Balthasar Methodological Considerations', *Theological Studies*, 58.1 (1997), pp. 61-84; p. 64
13. There, in two sentences, is the argument of Michael Buckley's magisterial study, *At the Origins of Modern Atheism* (New Haven and London: Yale University Press, 1987)

this lecture) as a matter of inculcation in the craft of biblical interpretation, of initiation into the unfathomable mystery that is God's holy wisdom, is to situate oneself in the tradition best summed up in Anselm's slogan: *Fides quaerens intellectum*.

For Thomas Aquinas (who also stood in that tradition), 'the belief that God exists' does not form part of Christian faith.[14] Christian faith, as Aquinas understood it, is a matter of believing God, which entails believing this or that on God's authority. Now, to believe on God's authority that God exists, really does not make much sense! Hence, his response to the suggestion that God's existence is an article of faith is to insist that truths such as 'God exists' are not articles of faith, but 'preambles to the articles', *preambula ad articulos*.[15] By this he did not mean that they are things that you have to establish before you can have faith, but, rather, that they are things which faith simply takes for granted.

*Fides quaerens intellectum*: the specific aim of theology 'in direct speech' is not 'explanation' but 'understanding'. This is at once an astonishingly bold assertion, and a soberingly modest one. It is bold in its insistence that, by God's gift, we are enabled to have some understanding of the unfathomable mystery which, in the last line of the *Divine Comedy*, Dante calls: *l'amor che muove il sole e l'altre stelle*, 'the love that moves the sun and the other stars'. It is the boldness of Aquinas's assertion that what he called 'the theology which pertains to holy teaching' – to God's teaching, God's 'doctrine' of God's self – is 'a kind of imprint on us of God's own knowledge, which is the single and simple grasp of everything': *una et simplex omnium [scientia]*.[16]

It is a modest assertion in its recognition that such understanding as we may attain, in heaven let alone on earth, amounts to nothing set against the One it seeks to understand.

Weber, in the lecture that I mentioned earlier, said that part of the social value of science and scholarship consists in helping us to 'gain clarity'.[17] And according to Karl Rahner, 'the answer

14. See John Jenkins, *Knowledge and Faith in Thomas Aquinas* (Cambridge: Cambridge University Press, 1997), p. 162
15. *Summa Theologiae*, 1a, 2. 2. ad 1
16. *Summa Theologiae*, 1a, 1. 4. ad 2
17. Weber, 'Science as a Vocation', p. 151

given in revelation *clarifies* the question [someone] asks'.[18]
*Clarifies*, throws some light upon. Understanding, unlike explanation, has no end. There is always so much more to see.
'To grasp God as the incomprehensible,' said Rahner in that essay on *Wissenschaft als 'Konfession'?*, 'inexpressibly transcending all our affirmations, that is a grace and blessing which is purchased at the cost of the desolation of wandering in shadows and images, as the great Newman had inscribed on his grave: 'To be able to stammer about God is after all more important than to speak exactly about the world.'[19]

Now, what kind of question would it be to which the appropriate response took the form of 'clarification', of throwing some light upon? The answer, presumably, is: a question asked in darkness. *Nel mezzo del camin di nostra vita*; in the middle of the journey of our life – it is on Good Friday that Dante finds himself in that 'dark wood' with which the *Divine Comedy* begins.

*Which Way Round?*
My brief remarks, a little earlier, about so-called 'proofs of God's existence', may have had you wondering: 'Is this some kind of card trick?' To set your minds at rest, I would now like to make one or two remarks about our uses of the word 'god'.

1. Two ways of using the word 'god'
Vastly to oversimplify matters, we could say that, in the history of Western culture, the word 'god' (and its cognates: 'Qeos', 'deus', 'dieu', 'Gott', and so on) has been used in two ways, one of which is helpful, and one of which is not.
[1] Your 'god' is what you worship
The helpful way, which was also the dominant use until the dawning of modernity, was to use the word in somewhat the same way that we use the word 'treasure'. A 'treasure' is what someone treasures, what someone values, and I do not know what you value until I find out by asking you and observing

---

18. Karl Rahner, 'The Foundation of Belief Today', *Theological Investigations* XVI, trans. David Morland (London: Darton, Longman and Todd, 1979), p. 9
19. Rahner, 'Science as a "Confession"?', pp. 394-5. (The motto on Newman's grave is: *ex umbris et imaginibus ad veritatem*.)

your behaviour. 'Treasure', then, is not the name of an entity or
class of entities – as 'vegetable', 'nation', 'ghost' or 'carpet' are –
it is one term of a relation: the relation of valuing.

Similarly, the word 'god' names, not an entity or class of entities, but whatever a group or individual worships, has their
heart set on, would (at least in principle, and *in extremis*) be will-
ing to die for. And I do not know what you worship – it may be
yourself, your nation, late capitalism or ice cream – until I find
out by asking you and observing your behaviour. 'God', in other
words, is not the name of an entity or class of entities; it indicates
the term of a relation: the relation of worshipping.

On this account, Christianity (not unlike Judaism and Islam)
is a kind of school in which people learn to worship, while yet
learning not to worship themselves, the world, or any of its con-
stituents; in which, to put it slightly differently, people learn to
worship the world's creator through learning not to worship
creatures; a school in which (to use the language of Paul's Letter
to the Romans, which Augustine picks up in *De Doctrina Christiana*) we learn to worship only the one 'from whom, and through
whom, and in whom' all things are.[20]

[2] A 'God' is a being of a particular kind, namely a divine
kind.

The unhelpful way of using the word 'god', which has come
to dominate discussion in modern Western culture, is to take it
be the name of an unusual class of entities. 'Theists' are people
who think this class has actual members ('monotheists' think
that it has one member; 'polytheists' think that it has many),
while 'atheists' think the class is empty. (All these words, incid-
entally, were invented, first in French and then in English, in the
late sixteenth and early seventeenth centuries.)

On this account, Christianity is a religion whose members believe there to be one 'God', of a rather complicated kind: they
will tell you that their God has a Son and sends a Spirit, although they will usually overlook these complications when
talking to natural scientists and members of other religions.

Preferring the older usage, I shall take 'the Christian doctrine
of God' to refer primarily to the process whereby people learn to
worship in the way that Christians do. What I am supposed to

20. *On Christian Teaching*, 1/10, p. 10. Cf. Romans 11.36: 'ex ... dia ... eis'.

be doing in this lecture is giving an account of this process, and of its point or content.

So: where should I begin? I said earlier that there is no one 'right' answer to this question. Nevertheless, is there not a kind of direction to the doctrine, a sense in which (for example) the Father comes 'before' the Son? Yes, but only a 'sense', and it is not a sense which would require any particular theologian, or school of theology, to begin their account at any particular point on the doctrinal 'map'.

2. Ways of thought

Medieval theology distinguished two *viae*, two 'roads' or 'ways' of thought, along which we might travel. The way, or order, in which we find things out is not necessarily the order in which, having found them out, we think them.

Thus, when we recite the Creed, we confess our faith in the three ways that we know God to be: we confess our faith in 'Father', 'Son', and 'Spirit'; in God as 'Creator', 'Redeemer', and 'Sanctifier'. But if you look at the next three headings on the outline, in which I refer to the 'Coming', the 'Appearance', and the 'Silence' of God, you will see that the three articles now run the other way – that I shall treat the third article before the second, and the second before the first – because, by and large, that is the order in which we learn appropriately to worship; the order in which we come to understand something of who God is: only in the Spirit do we hear the Word.

*The Coming of God*

And now, at last, after all that preparatory work, I am in a position briefly to comment on the three ways in which, as Christians, we learn to understand the holy mystery of God.

In the first place, then, Christians confess their faith in God as 'Holy Spirit'. Nowhere is it more important than here to remember that Christian doctrine is a matter of biblical interpretation. If we forget that calling God 'spirit' is a kind of footnote – referring us to an immensely varied range of biblical images and metaphors – we shall be in danger of assuming that the sense of the title is more or less self-evident, because 'everybody knows', do they not, that 'gods' are 'spirits'?

But what, for goodness' sake, is a 'spirit'? Is God like a ghost, or more like vodka? Oh, I see: what's important about 'spirit' is that it is *immaterial*. Is God, then, something like the square root of minus one?

It is far from obvious what kind of thing a 'spirit' is, but this need not concern us because, to call God 'Holy Spirit' is not to say what kind of thing God is, for God is not a thing of *any* kind, not even a divine or 'spiritual' kind.

Calling God 'Holy Spirit' does two things: it acknowledges the vitality of God's constitutive indwelling of every fact, and thing, and feature of the world – *Veni, Creator Spiritus*, and it celebrates, in the poetry of 'wind' and 'breath', the uncontrollability of grace: the forms of which may vary from the gentle breeze Elijah felt[21] to the devastating storm-winds of God's justice.

Moreover, according to the classic principle that the three that Christianity confesses God to be are only to be distinguished from each other in terms of the relationships of origin that they are said to be ('parent' from 'child'; 'utterer' from 'utterance', or 'word', and so on) then, since 'Holy Spirit' names no such relation, it is not, in fact, a name proper to the third person of the Trinity. I am happy to keep company with Augustine and Aquinas, who settled for 'love', or 'gift', as the least misleading candidates for naming this 'face' of our experience of God.

*Ubi caritas et amor, Deus ibi est*; where is love and lovingkindness, there is God. Unless we learn to name God thus, we shall not learn what else is to be said of God. Where is love and lovingkindness, there is God. Misread this, and it sounds like sentimental pious evasion of the pain and darkness of the world. But, as the great 'prophetic' movements of contemporary theology – liberation theology, feminist theology, 'green' theologies, and so on – have powerfully reminded us, this doctrine of God's generosity, God's endlessly enlivening self-bestowal, is best interpreted from the standpoint of the victims. 'Spirit' is not where materialists go at weekends for refreshment; it is the principle of their subversion.

I hinted, just now, that the doctrine of God as Holy Spirit, of God as gift, as grace, is a doctrine of our *experience* of God. Not, I

---

21. See 1 Kings 19:9-18

hasten to add, a doctrine of 'religious experience'. Theories of 'religious experience' are theories as to why it may or may not be appropriate to call certain experiences of a particular kind 'religious', whereas to speak of God, the mystery of the world, the world's creator, as 'grace', is to construe everything there is, everything that we do and undergo, as God-given, graced, enabled and enlivened by the breath of God. *All* our experience is the inextricable interweaving of experience of grace, and of its dark refusal: the destructive obstinacy which we call sin.

Karl Rahner made the point succinctly: 'the possibility of experiencing grace, and the possibility of experiencing grace *as* grace, are not the same thing'.[22]

The laborious pedagogy of Christian discipleship, the schooling in which we learn to worship God, and God alone, is a matter of learning to 'discern the Spirit'.

The doctrine of God as Holy Spirit, of God's gracious inhabitation of the world, indicates, we might say, the 'atmosphere' in which Christians do their politics and ethics and aesthetics: an atmosphere resistant, for example, to doctrines of fate and blind necessity. But, of course, our politics and ethics and aesthetics will only be *well* done in the measure of our alertness to God's utterance, our attentiveness to the forms of God's appearance in the world, for it is amongst the forms of God's appearance that we seek the *criteria* according to which the discernment of spirits is best made.

### The Appearance of God
The forms of God's appearance are not God. As *forms* - as sights, or sounds, or shapes; as people or ideas, events or institutions – they are creatures. (This observation is, once again, 'grammatical'!) According to the Christian doctrine of God, the final, focal and definitive form of God's appearance is Jesus Christ, the Word made flesh. The flesh, the man that Jesus is, is human; but the Word that Jesus is is God.

According to Karl Rahner: 'When God wills to be non-divine,

---

22. Rahner, 'Concerning the Relationship between Nature and Grace', *Theological Investigations* I, trans. Cornelius Ernst (London: Darton, Longman and Todd, 1961), p. 300

the human person comes to be.'23 Actually, that makes the point a little too strongly, because so brief a formula risks collapsing the tension set up by the identity between the Word that is 'in the beginning', the Word 'through whom all things are made', and the Word made flesh that 'dwelt among us'. We need to bear in mind that the Word made flesh in Jesus Christ is not the only form of God's appearance, not the only resonance of God's Word in the world.

(There is a fascinating passage in the *Summa* in which Aquinas, considering the question as to whether the multiplicity and diversity of creatures is due to God, argues that it is, on the grounds that no single creature could give God's goodness adequate expression: not even, by implication, the humanity of Christ!24)

In his *Foundations of Christian Faith*, Rahner has what is, to my mind, a rather better formulation of what he calls 'the innermost centre of the Christian understanding of existence', when he says: 'Man' – sorry about that, blame German syntax: 'humankind' will not quite do, because he also has one individual in mind: 'Adam', the earthling, and the new 'Adam', so, if you will bear with the translation: – 'Man is the event of a free, unmerited and forgiving, and absolute self-communication of God'.25 From which it follows, of course, that Jesus Christ is the only fully human human being that there is. Being divine, Christ is not less human than the rest of us, but more so. (By the way, 'Foundations' is a terrible translation of the German *Grundkurs*, which might be better rendered as 'five-finger exercises'. The issue is not unimportant, because many of Rahner's critics have, unwarrantedly, charged him with 'foundationalism': that is to say, with building his theology on the 'foundations' of his philosophy. This issue has, to my mind, been settled by a brilliant

23. Rahner, 'On the Theology of the Incarnation', *Theological Investigations IV. More Recent Writings*, trans. Kevin Smyth (London: DLT, 1966), p. 116, in the amended translation of George Vandevelde, 'The Grammar of Grace', *Theological Studies*, 49 (1988), p. 450

24. See Aquinas, *Summa Theologiae. Ia*, 47. I .c: 'quia per unam creaturam [suam bonitatem] sufficienter repraesentari non potest'

25. Rahner, *Foundations of Christian Faith. An Introduction to the Idea of Christianity*, Trans. William V. Dych (London: DLT, 1978), p. 116

recent study by Dr Karen Kilby, entitled *Karl Rahner. Theology and Philosophy*.[26])

It is, I said earlier, amongst the forms of God's appearance in the world that we seek the criteria according to which the discernment of spirits is best made. In a section of *Foundations* entitled 'Jesus Christ as the Criterion', Rahner says that it is 'only in him', the 'crucified and risen one', that 'a discernment of spirits in an ultimate sense is possible'.[27]

We are, after all, talking about travelling, about the process of Christian doctrine as the context in which we learn our way to God. A 'criterion' is a road-sign; it indicates the way we are to go.

*The Silence of God*

Now that we are nearly at the end, we can move towards the beginning, towards the 'arch', or the 'first' in God: to God addressed by Jesus, even in the darkness of Gethesmane, as 'Father'. (I am sure that you will have heard sermons in which the preacher made sentimental noises about the *intimacy* of Jesus' relationship with the Father, pointing out that he uses the word 'abba', usually rendered as 'daddy'. What such preachers usually do *not* mention is that the only occasion on which Jesus is said to use this word is in the Garden of Gethsemane.)

According to Christian doctrine, God, the Holy One, 'the mystery of the world', is *experienced* as love's gift, *interpreted* as Jesus Christ, and *acknowledged* as absolutely beyond our comprehension.

Not everything that can be understood can be imagined (if you doubt this, try imagining the square root of 93 – which is, of course, perfectly intelligible; in case you had forgotten, it is 9.6436508). But that which is beyond our understanding is, *a fortiori*, beyond imagining. And yet, believers and non-believers alike persist in speaking as though we could gain some imaginative purchase on what we are saying when we speak of God.

Philip said to him, "Lord, show us the Father, and we shall be satisfied." Jesus said to him, "Have I been with you so long,

26. Karen Kilby, *Karl Rahner. Theology and Philosophy* (London: Routledge, 2004)
27. Rahner, *Foundations*, p. 157

and yet you do not know me, Philip? He who has seen me has seen the Father."[28]

It is, of course, perfectly possible to gaze upon the figure of the crucified without 'seeing' Jesus. 'Seeing', in the fourth gospel, is a metaphor for understanding, for 'seeing the point'. To 'see' Jesus is to know him to be the Christ, the form of God's appearance. Therefore, in seeing him, we see the One who sends him. There is, to put it crudely, nothing 'behind' the figure of the crucified on which to rest our gaze.

But does not Jesus speak of 'seeing' the Father? Yes, indeed, but attentiveness to the way in which this metaphor works takes us into the very heart of trinitarian doctrine.

'The Son can do nothing of his own accord, but only what he *sees* the Father doing' (that's John, Chapter 5).[29] And here are two glosses, by Saint Augustine, on that quotation: 'The way in which the Son sees the Father is simply by *being* the Son'; or, again: 'In seeing he is born, and in being born he sees': *Videndo enim natus est, et nascendo videt.*[30]

But if 'seeing' the Father is, for God's eternal Son, the fruit of his obedient existence, of his existence as pure 'from-the-Fatherness', then presumably something similar is to be said about adopted sonship: namely, that such 'seeing' of the Father as we may be made capable of will be the fruit, rather than the precondition, of our life's obedience.

To grow in the knowledge of God is to move into ever deeper darkness. This view of things, commonplace in Christianity for three-quarters of its history, is difficult to communicate in a society, such as ours, which, on the one hand, has largely discarded what it supposes to be traditional Christian belief, on the grounds that such belief is not only fictional but infantile, while, on the other, exhibiting a thirsty fascination with the imagined delights of 'spirituality', and with every kind of superstition – from astrology to newly invented forms of 'oriental mysticism'.

Traditional Christianity was more adult and more realistic in its insistence that darkness is the shape and texture of our jour-

28. John 14:8-9
29. John 5:19
30. Augustine, *The Trinity*, Bk. ii. 3; *In Joann. Ev.* (CCSL, 36), xxxi, 4; see Nicholas Lash, *Believing Three Ways in One God*, p. 49

ney into God. It is, said John of the Cross, a 'serious imperfection' to 'desire to feel God and taste of him as if he were comprehensible and accessible'.[31]

There is nothing exotic about this insistence that 'the reality of the divine' is, in Denys Turner's phrase, 'a language-defeating silence'.[32] It was the common wisdom of traditions which, not having yet invented 'religion' as a therapy or pastime on the margins of the real world, knew how to correlate reverence for the mystery of God with the darkness shaped by the pain, and confusion, and unmeaning of the world.

That the first word, and the last, of everything, and of the entire story of the world, is 'love', or 'peace', is not self-evident; nor is it an illusion cherished by those who cannot bear the bleakness of the world. It is, as true, perpetually astonishing, subversive, counterfactual. Which, of course, brings us back to grace and the doctrine of the given Spirit, with which we began. The Christian doctrine of God's Trinity is a process of unceasing, self-corrective movement.

*A School of Friendship*

Following in Augustine's footsteps, I have been at pains to emphasise that the Christian doctrine of God is a pedagogical *process* more fundamentally than it is what, *in* this process, is taught, communicated, shared. To put it slightly differently, Christian teaching, like all teaching, takes place in a school (another 'grammatical' remark). And the name given to the school in which this teaching takes place is an 'assembled', 'gathered' people: a 'church'.

As Vatican II ended, several of the bishops who took part told me that the most important lesson they had learnt, through the conciliar process, had been a renewed recognition that the church exists to be, for all its members, a school of lifelong education: a school of holiness and wisdom, a school of *friendship* (a much better rendering of *caritas* than 'charity' would be).

---

31. John of the Cross, *The Dark Night of the Soul*, 1 6. 5 (quoted from Denys Turner, *The Darkness of God. Negativity in Christian Mysticism* (Cambridge: Cambridge University Press, 1995), p. 246
32. Turner, op. cit., p. 22

In other words, Christian teaching about 'church and sacraments' is not *supplementary* to the doctrine of God – as if we needed to learn about God and *also* about the church. It is the specification of the context in which the Christian doctrine of God occurs. I therefore welcome the emphasis placed by John Jenkins, in his study of Aquinas's views on 'holy teaching', on the notion of 'apprenticeship'.[33] Christianity is, or should be, a kind of workshop, the purpose of whose pedagogy is to wean us from idolatry and to purify desire.

*In the End*
I conclude with two footnotes, both about travelling.

In the first place, if the Christian doctrine of God does constitute a set of road-signs, then, at any point along the way, you do not know where you will end. The journey into understanding is every bit as dangerous as foreign travel used to be.

In the second place, the usual conclusion of the eucharist, in the Latin rite, was the deacon's announcement: *Ite, missa est*, from which announcement the entire celebration took its name: the 'Mass'. Although the matter was once in some dispute, today there is 'no doubt at all' that 'the original and basic meaning of the word *missa* was simply *dimissio*, 'dismissal'. *Ite, missa est* means neither more nor less than: 'The meeting is concluded.'[34] Nevertheless, it was not mere fancy but a remembrance of the common root of 'mission' and 'dismissal' in the verb 'to send' which gave generations of preachers licence to remind their gatherings, or 'congregations', that Christian teaching, the process of the Christian doctrine of God, always occurs between inheritance and proclamation, tradition and mission.

33. See Jenkins, op. cit., pp. 68, 218
34. See Joseph-André Jungmann, *Missarum Sollemnia. Explication géné-tique de la Messe romaine*, I (Paris: Aubier, 1956), p. 218

116

# The Contributors

GAVIN D'COSTA: Reader in Christian Theology, Bristol, England. He is the author of several books including *Theology and Religious Pluralism. The Challenge of Other Religions* (1986), *John Hick's Theology of Religions. A Critical Evaluation* (1987), *The Meeting of Religions and the Trinity* (2000), *Sexing the Trinity. Gender, Culture and the Divine* (2000).

DANIEL MADIGAN SJ: President of the recently established Institute for the Study of Religion and Cultures at the Gregorian University, Rome. He is the author of *The Qur'ân's Self-Image: Writing and Authority in Islam's Scripture* (2001).

JOSEPH FITZMYER SJ: Professor Emeritus of Biblical Studies at the Catholic University, Washington DC and a well known scholar of New Testament studies in the field of Aramaic Studies. Among his many publications are the *The Gospel According to Luke* (1982) and *Acts of the Apostles* (1998). He is co-editor of the *New Jerome Biblical Commentary* (1989). He was a member of the Pontifical Biblical Commission for many years.

GERALD O'COLLINS SJ: Professor Emeritus of Systematic Theology, Gregorian University, Rome. Among his many publications are *Fundamental Theology* (1981), *Jesus Risen* (1987), *Interpreting Jesus* (1993) and *Christology* (1995).

DERMOT A. LANE: President of Mater Dei Institute of Education, Dublin, Parish Priest of Balally, and a part-time lecturer in the Irish School of Ecumenics. He is the author of several books in theology including *Christ at the Centre* (1990), *Keeping Hope Alive* (1996) and is one of the editors of *The New Dictionary of Theology* (1987).

RAPHAEL GALLAGHER CSSR: Professor of Moral Theology at the Accademia Alfonsiana, Rome. He is a regular contributor on the Alphonsian tradition in moral theology. He is editor of *Catholic Medical Ethics: A Tradition which Progresses History and Conscience: Studies in Honour of Father Sean O'Riordan, CSsR* (1989).

CLARE MCGOVERN: Member of the Irish Sisters of Mercy, President of the Regina Mundi Institute, Rome and Lecturer in Systematic Theology.

LIAM BERGIN: Priest of the Diocese of Ossory, Rector of the Pontifical Irish College and Lecturer in Sacramental Theology at the Gregorian University Rome. He is the author of *O Propheticum Lavacrum: Baptism as Symbolic Act of Eschatological Salvation* (1999).

NICHOLAS LASH: Fellow of Clare Hall and Emeritus Norris-Hulse Professor of Divinity at the University of Cambridge. He has the distinction of being the first Catholic to hold a chair in Divinity at Cambridge since the Reformation. He is a prolific writer of articles and books, including *Theology on Dover Beach, Easter in the Ordinary, Believing Three Ways in One God* and *The Beginning and End of Religion*.